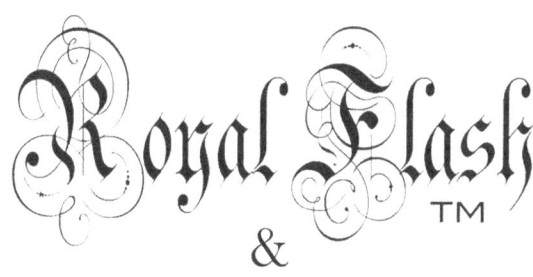

&

Cort's Royal Ink Tattoo Company
Presents

"Book of Advanced Theory

Mandala Designs"

All artwork by

Cort Bengtson

Published by Cort's Royal Ink Tattoo Company
Book Design and Layout by Cort Bengtson

Copyright 2017
All images are on file with
The Library of Congress

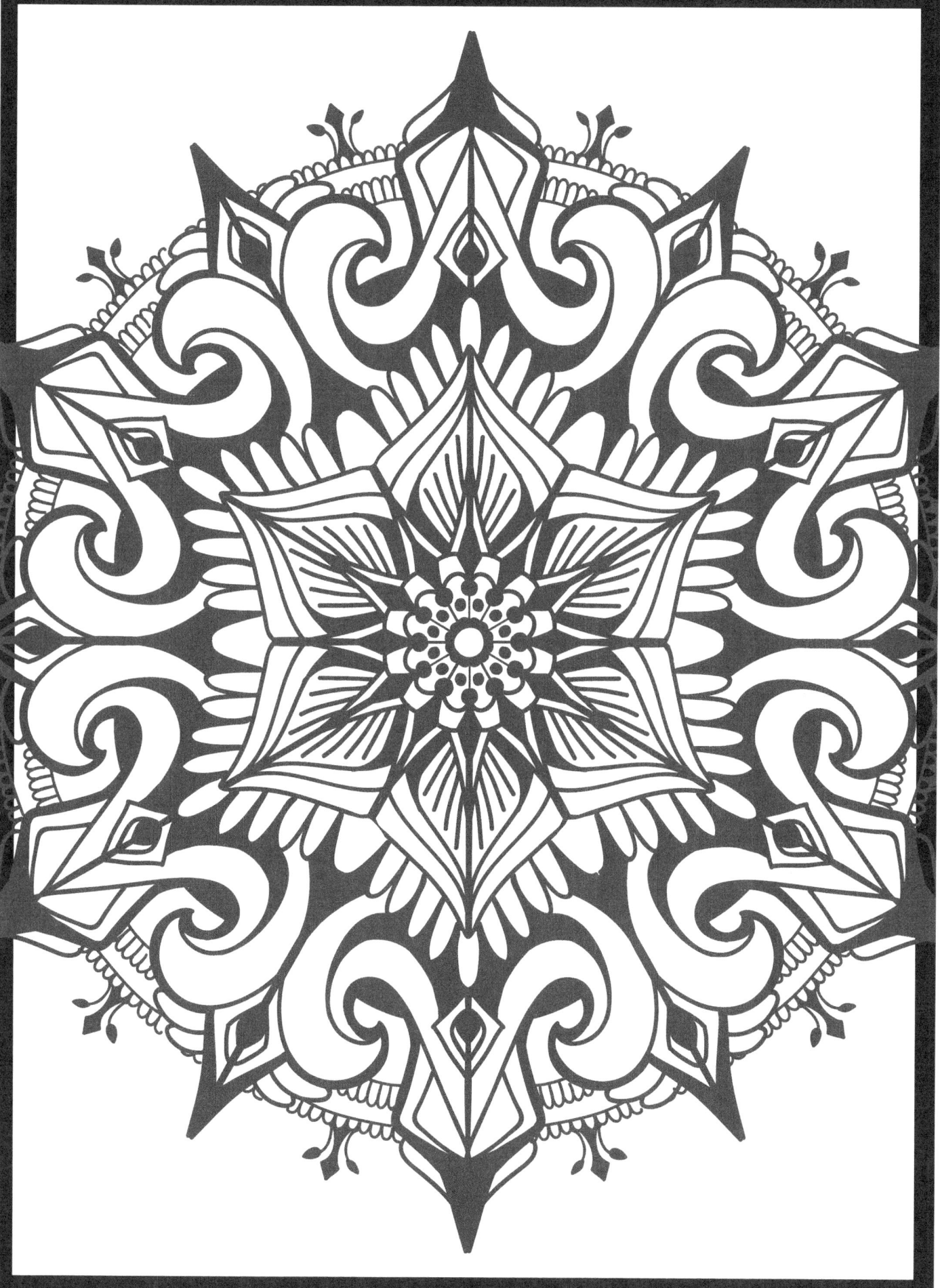

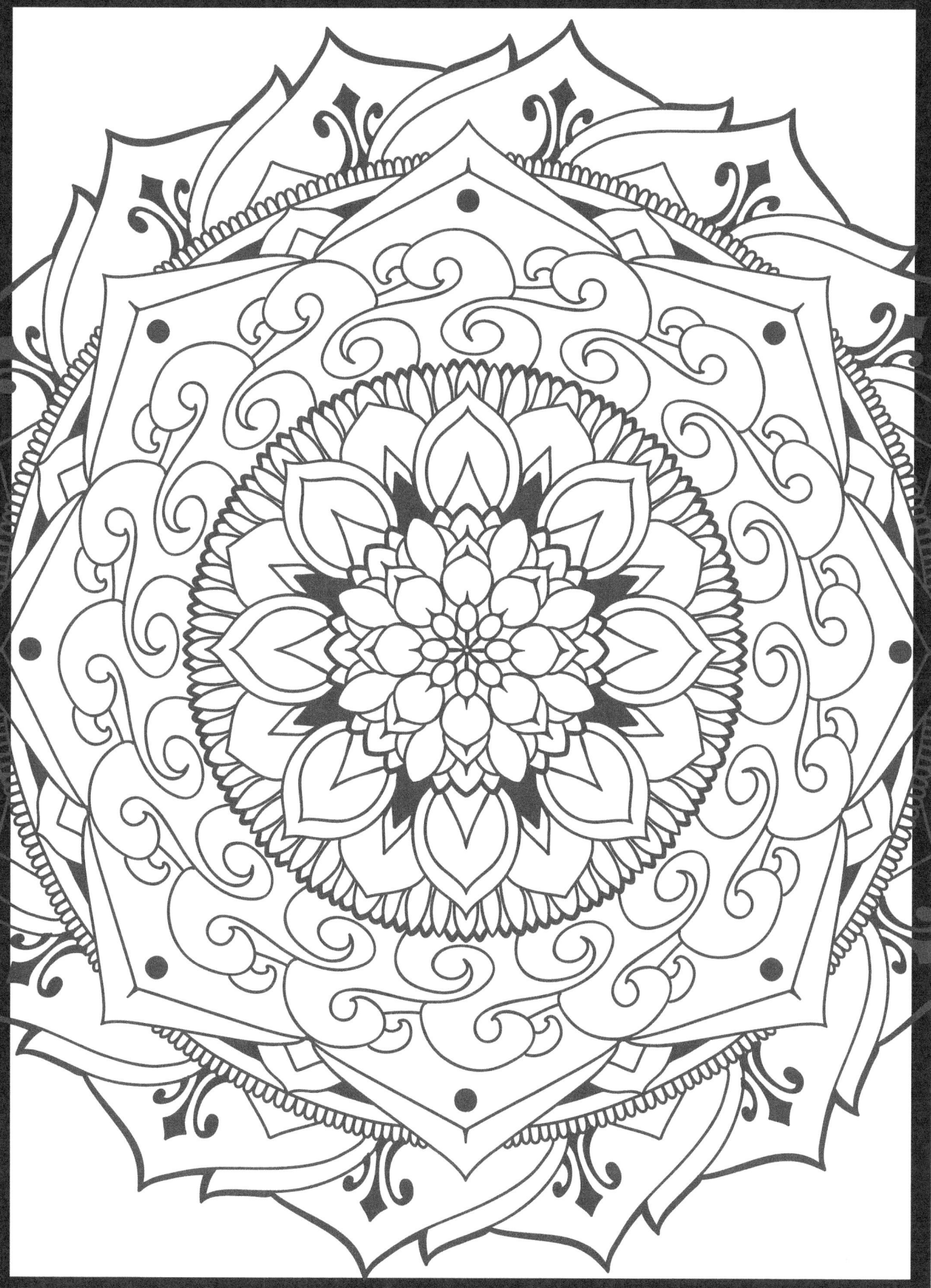

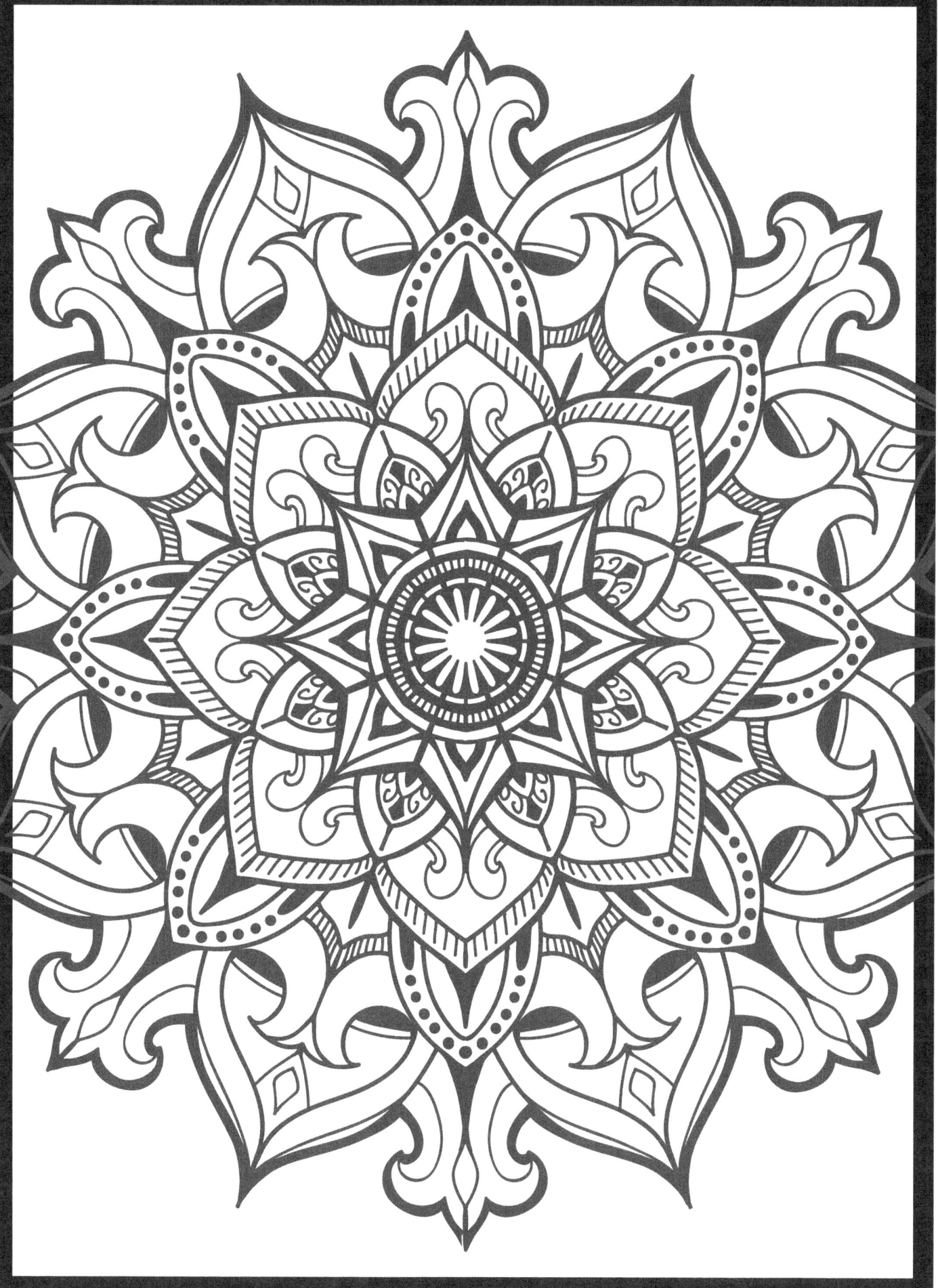

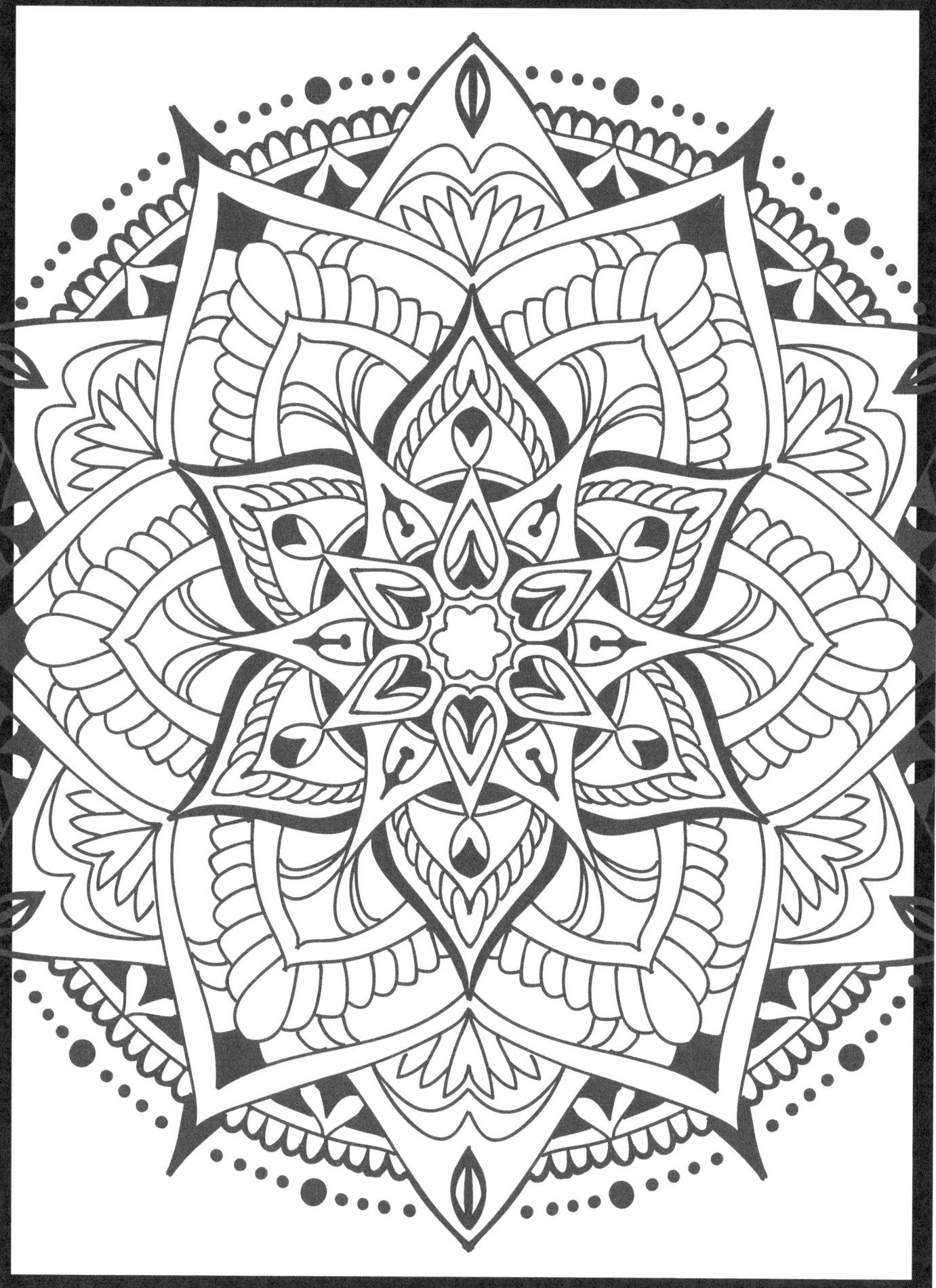

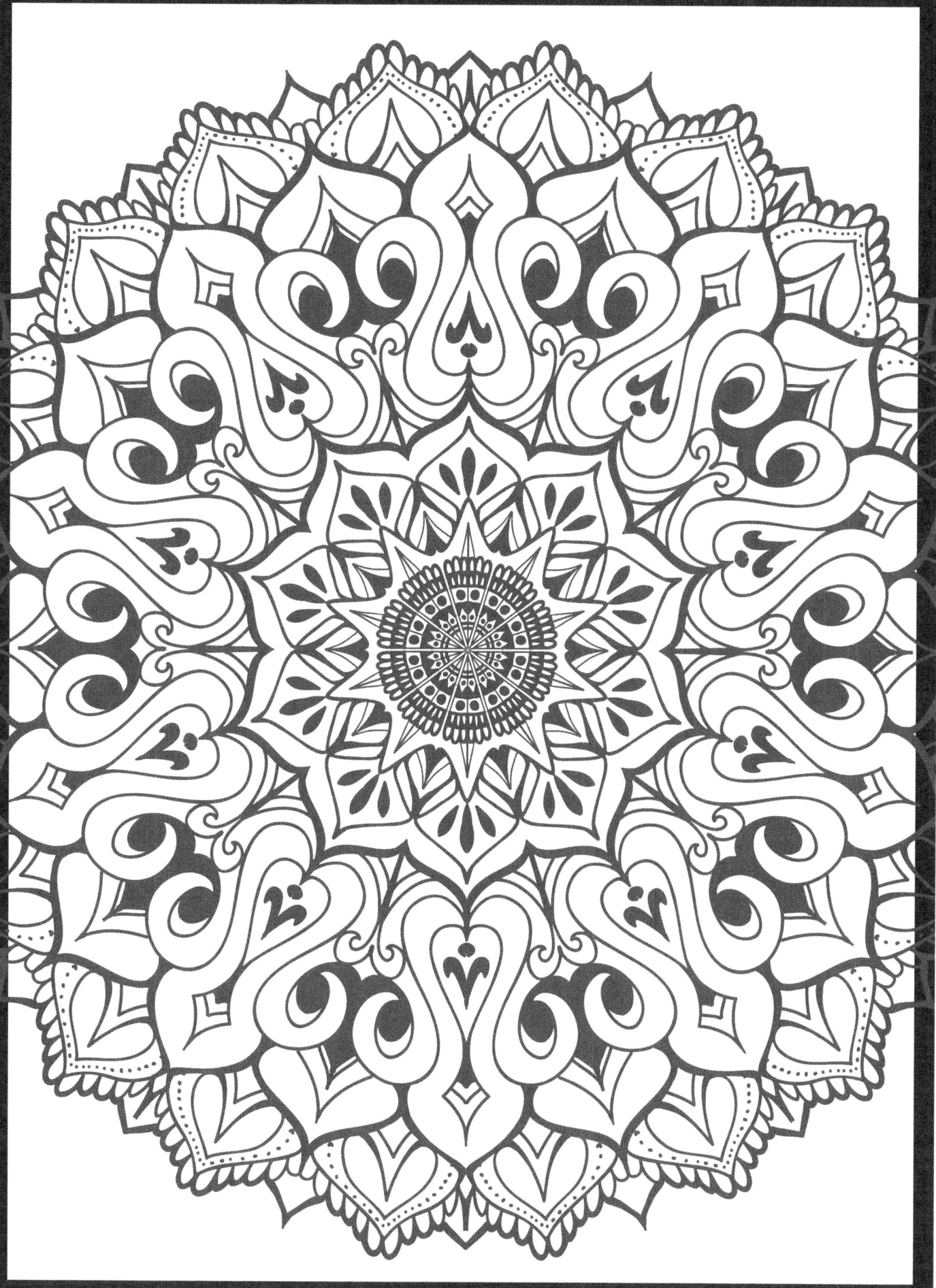

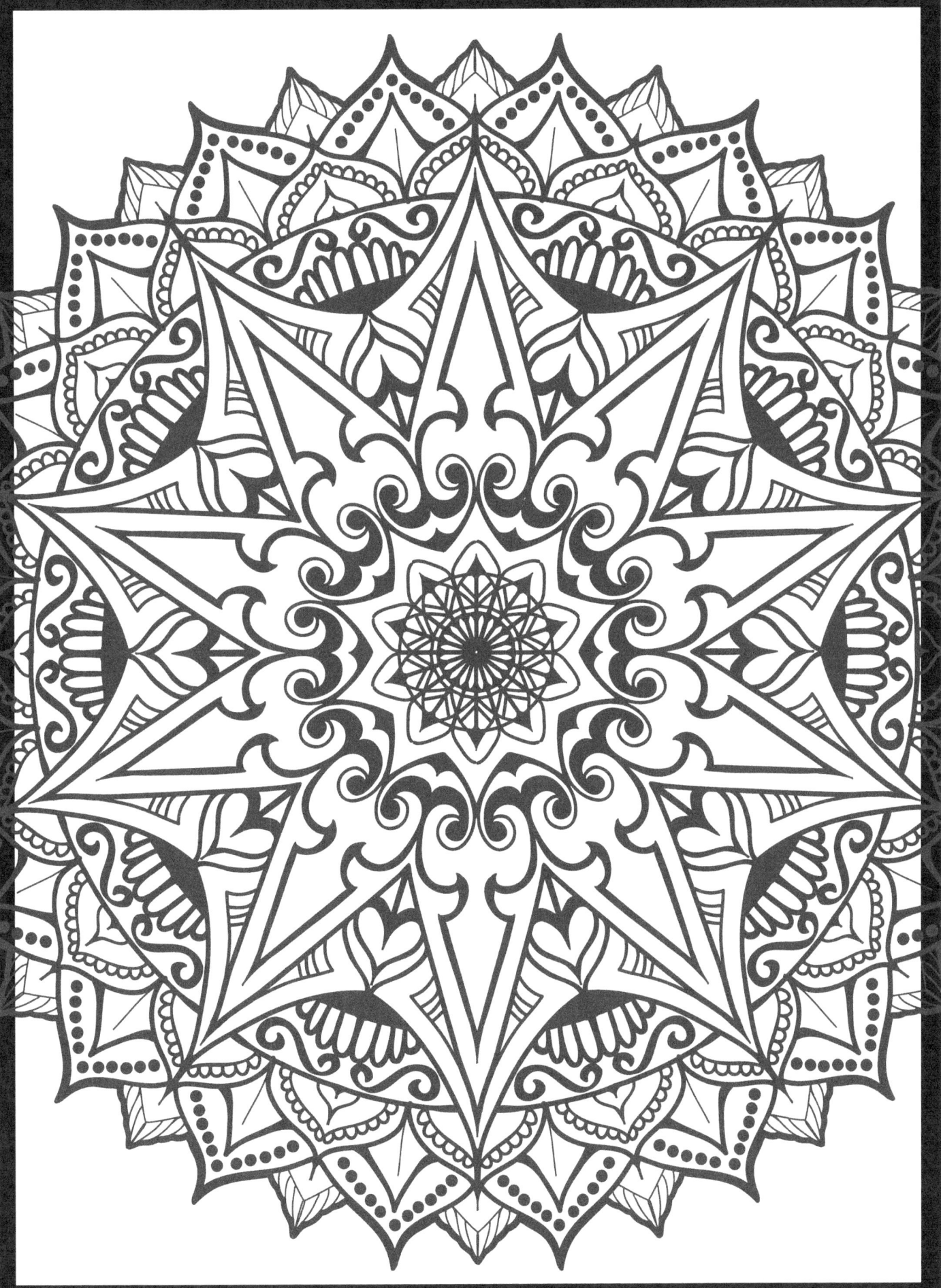

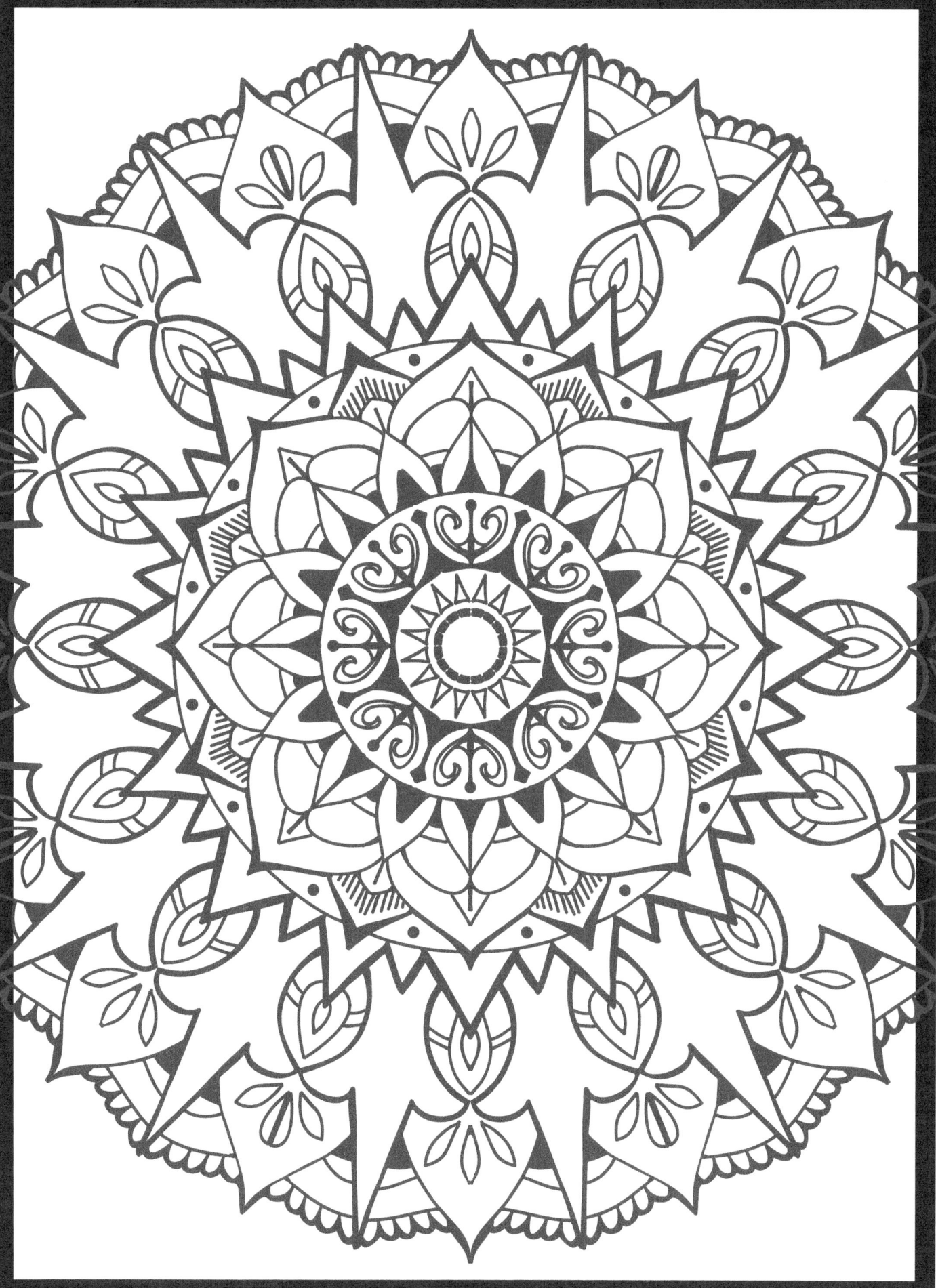

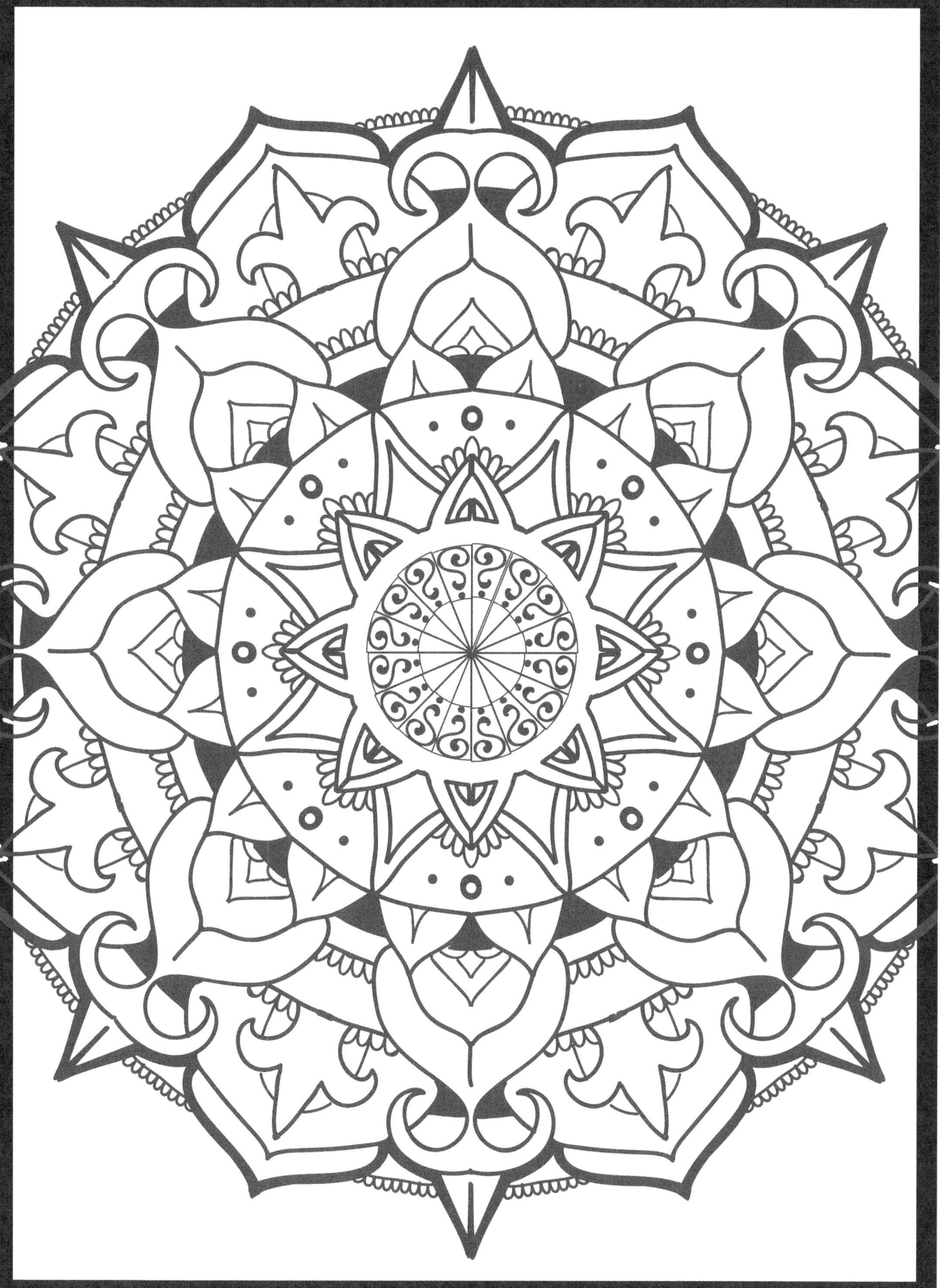

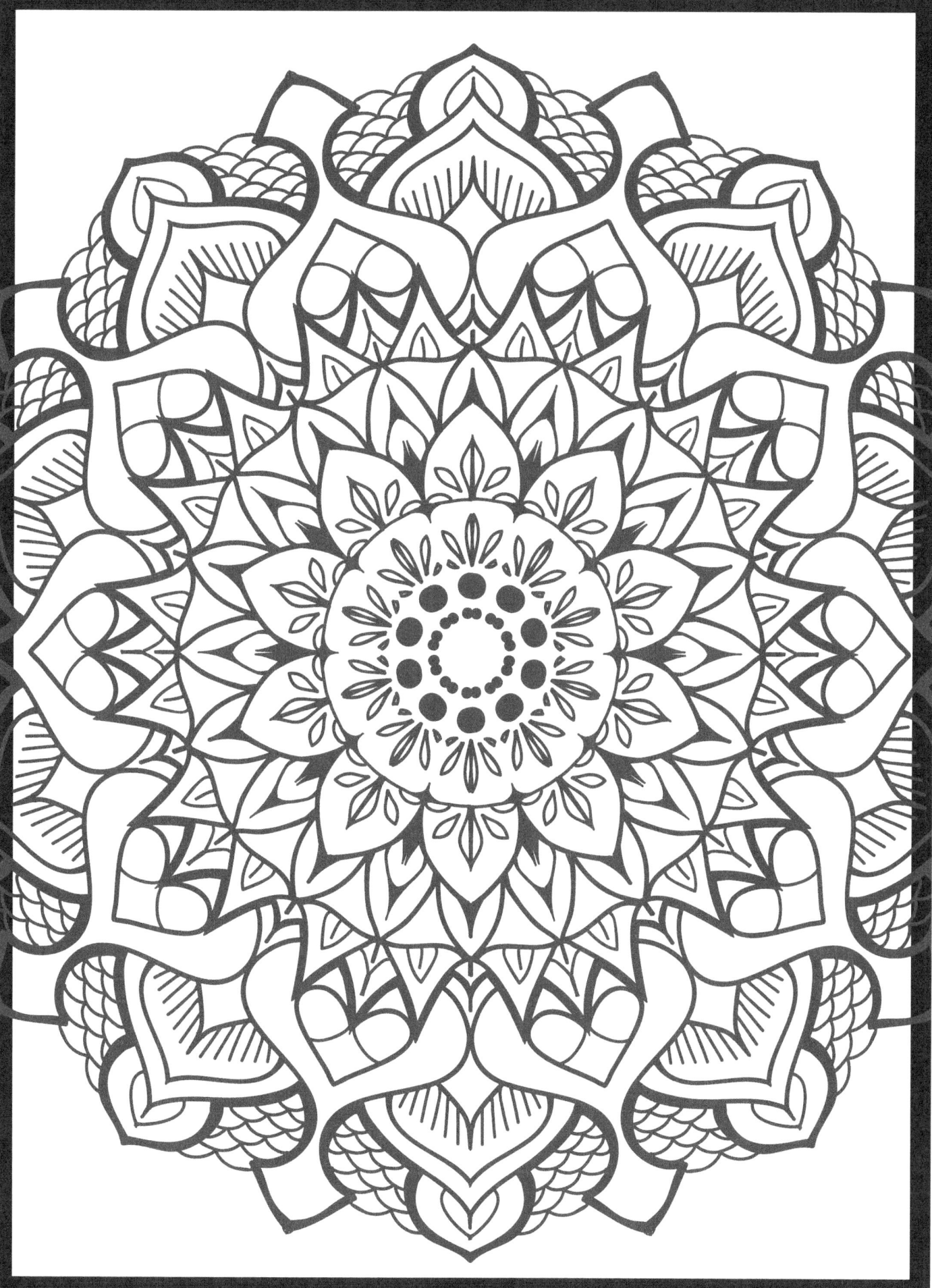

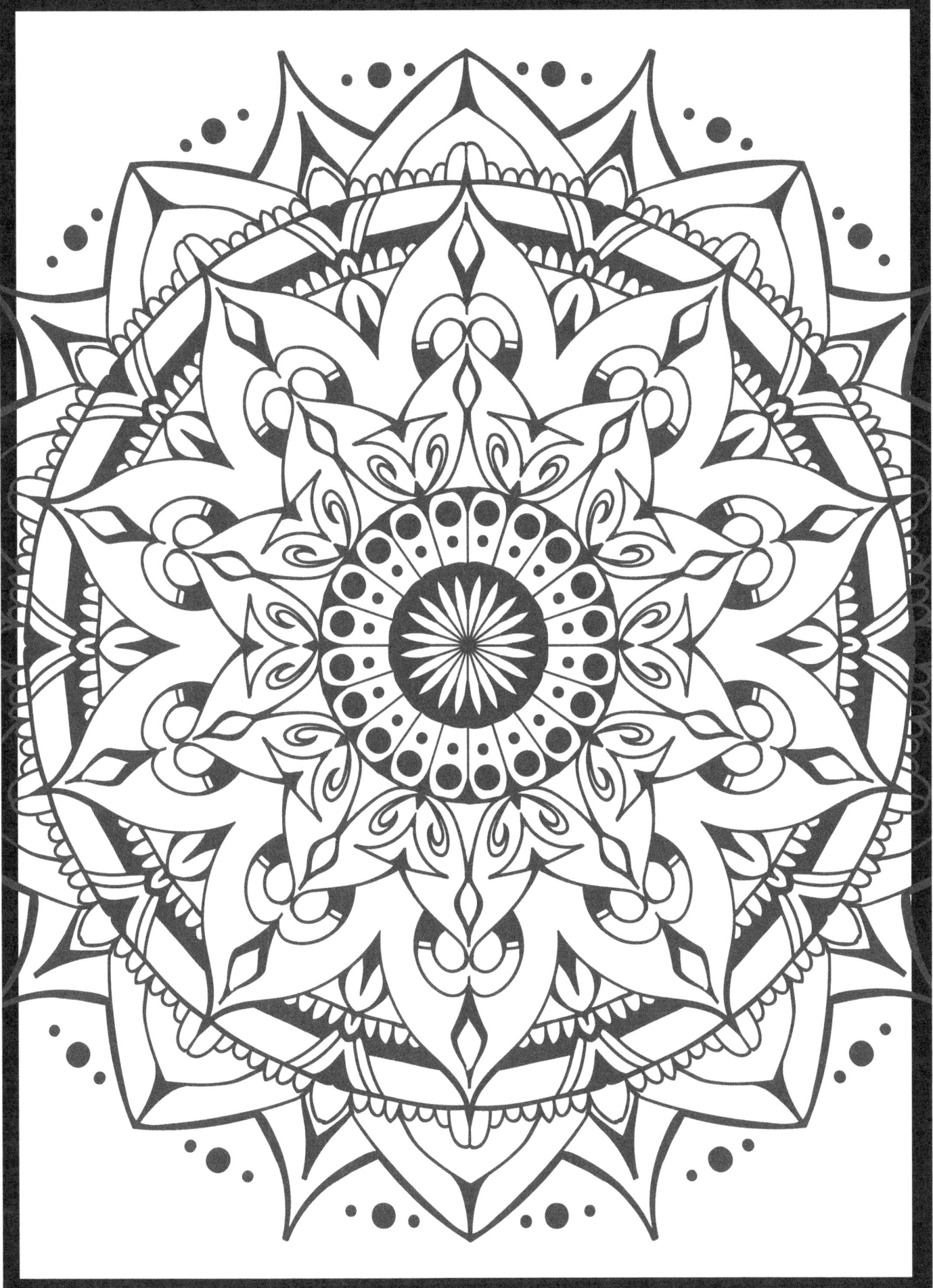

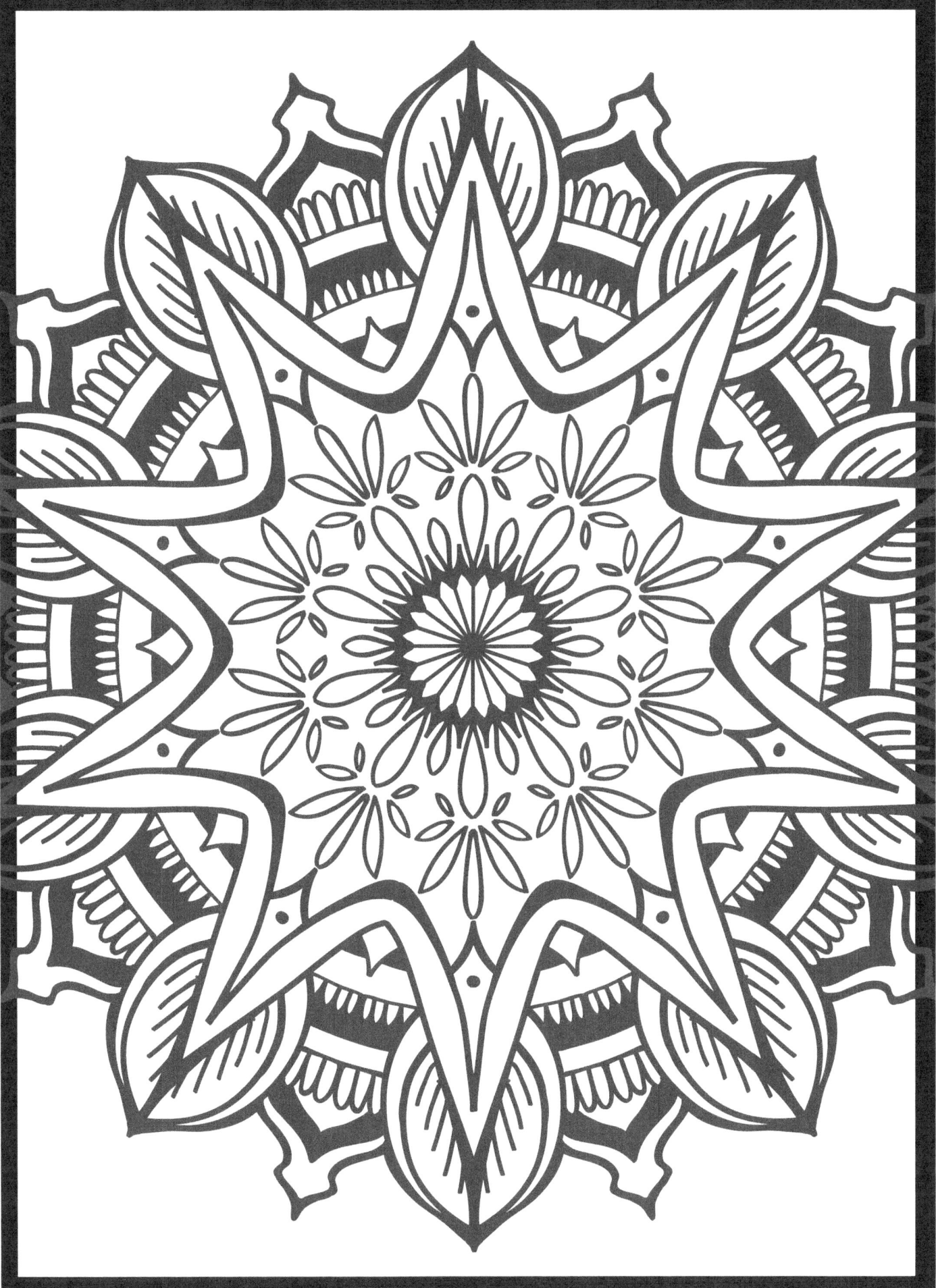

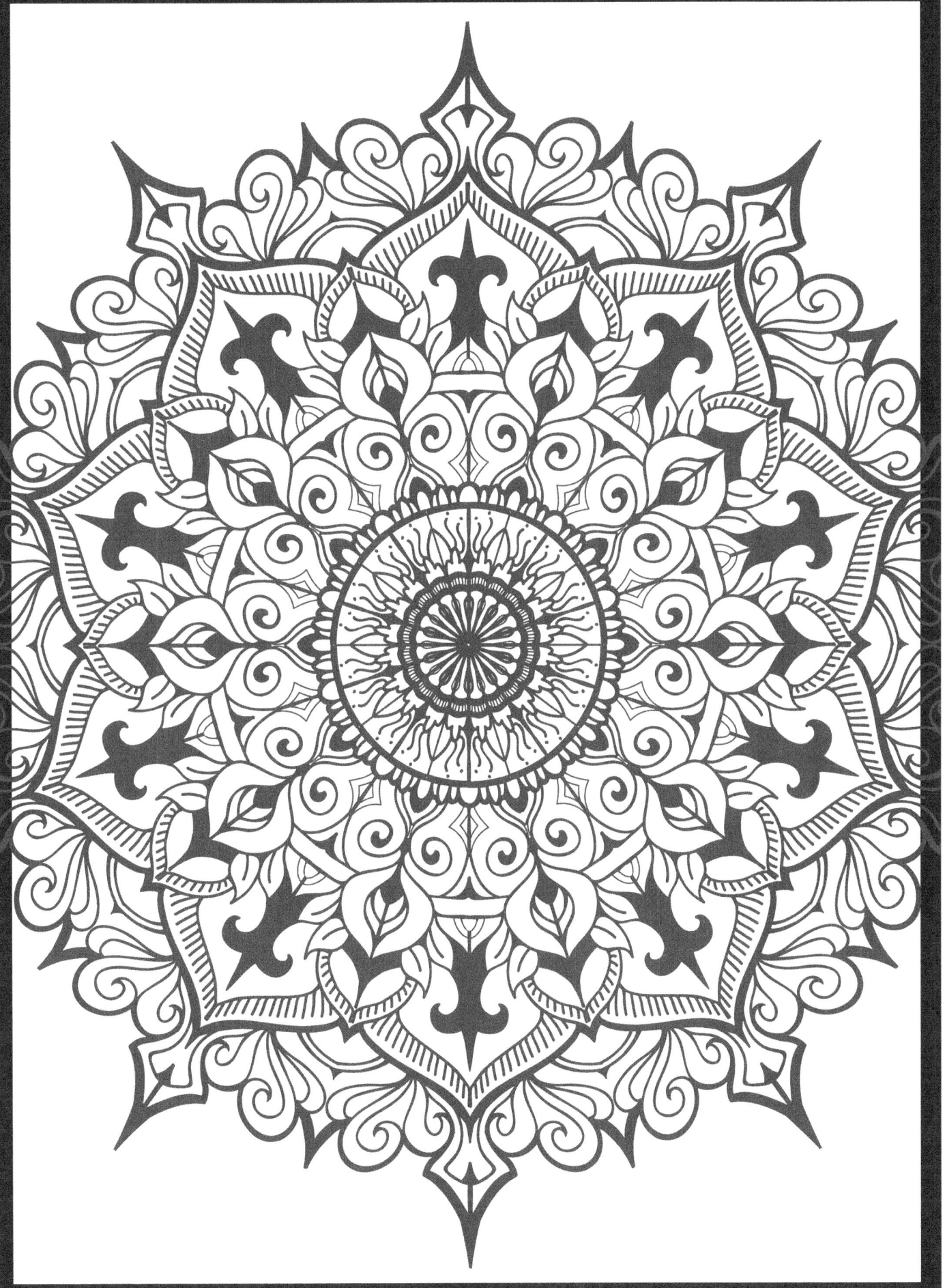

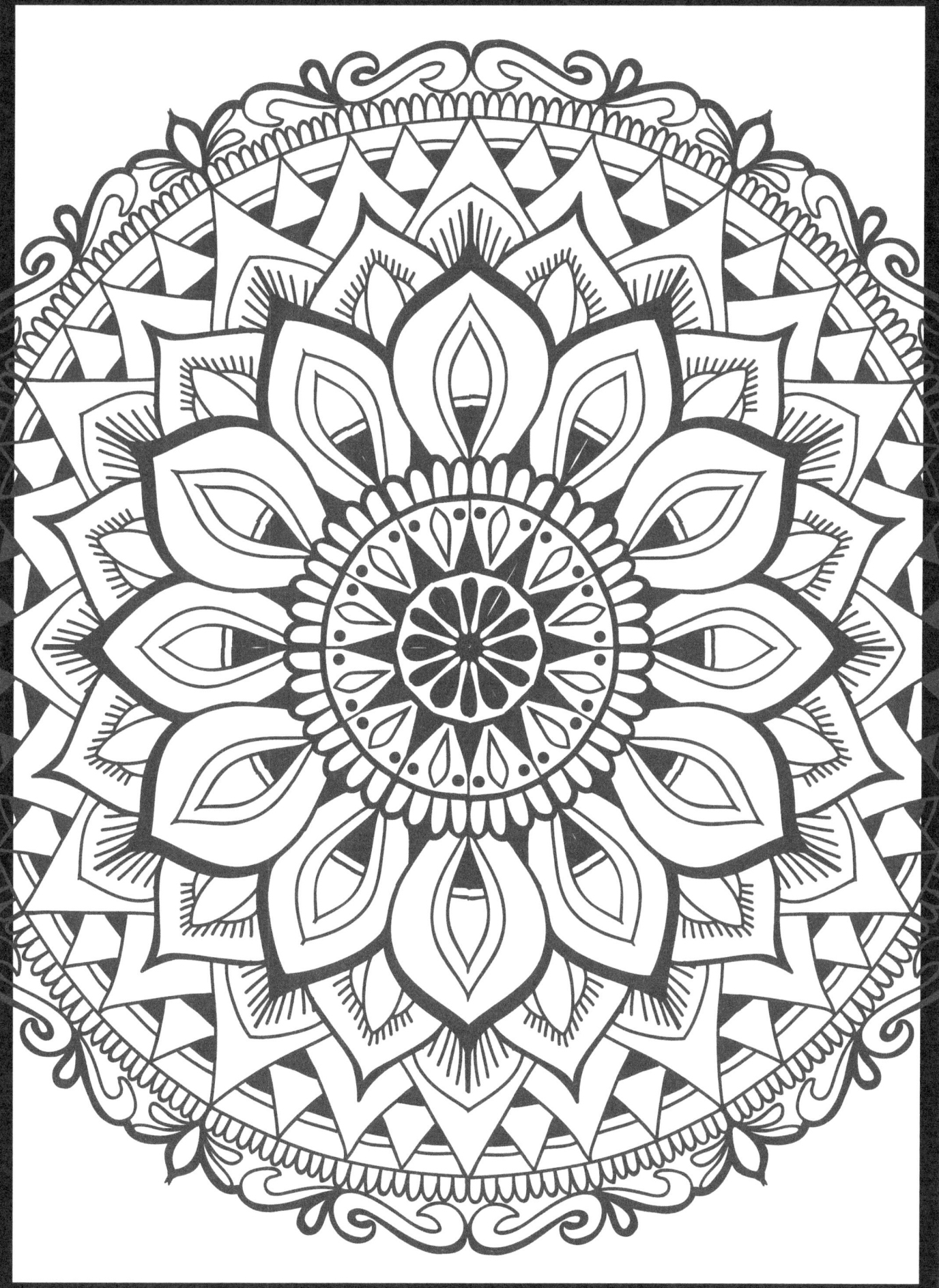

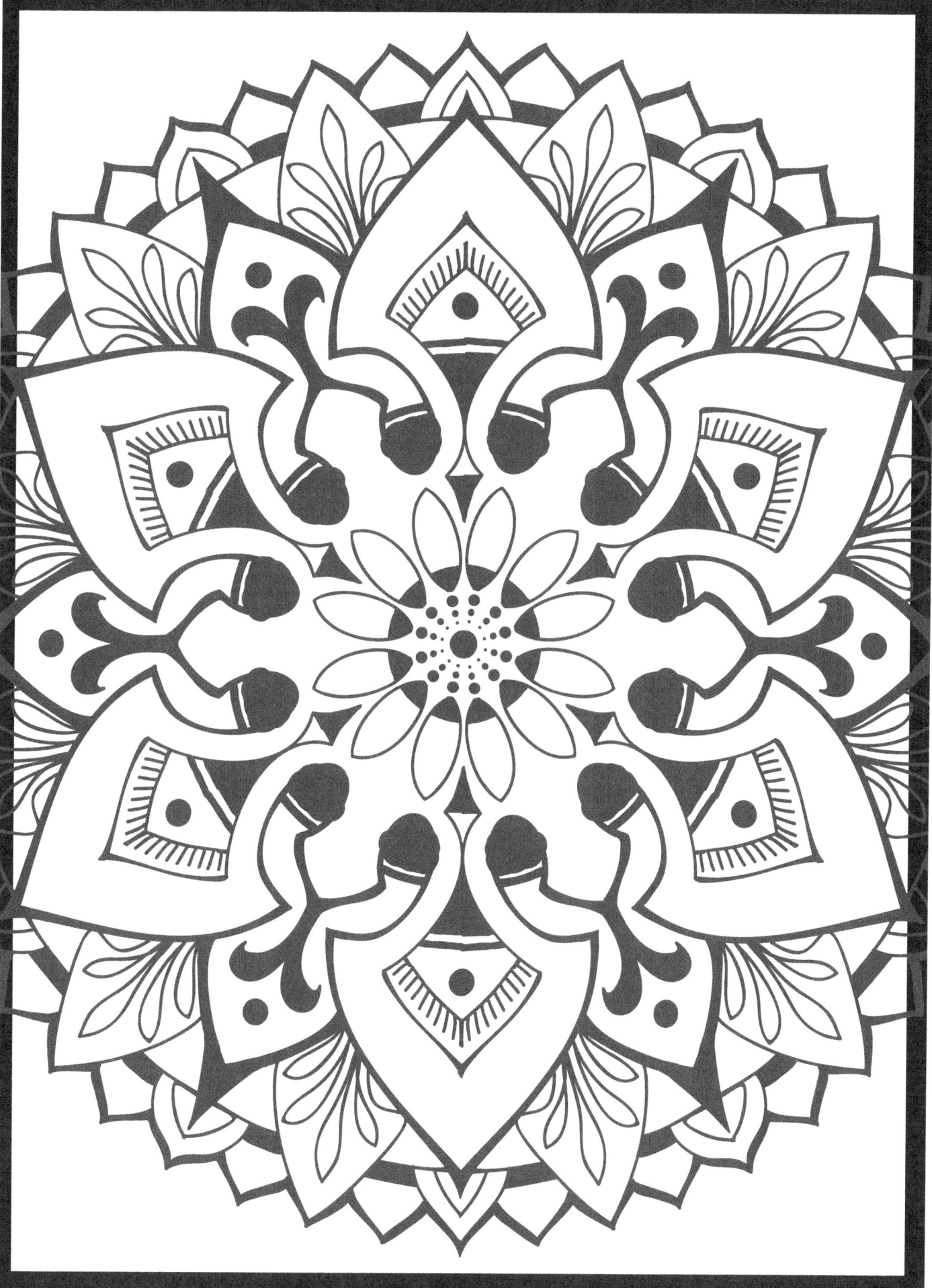

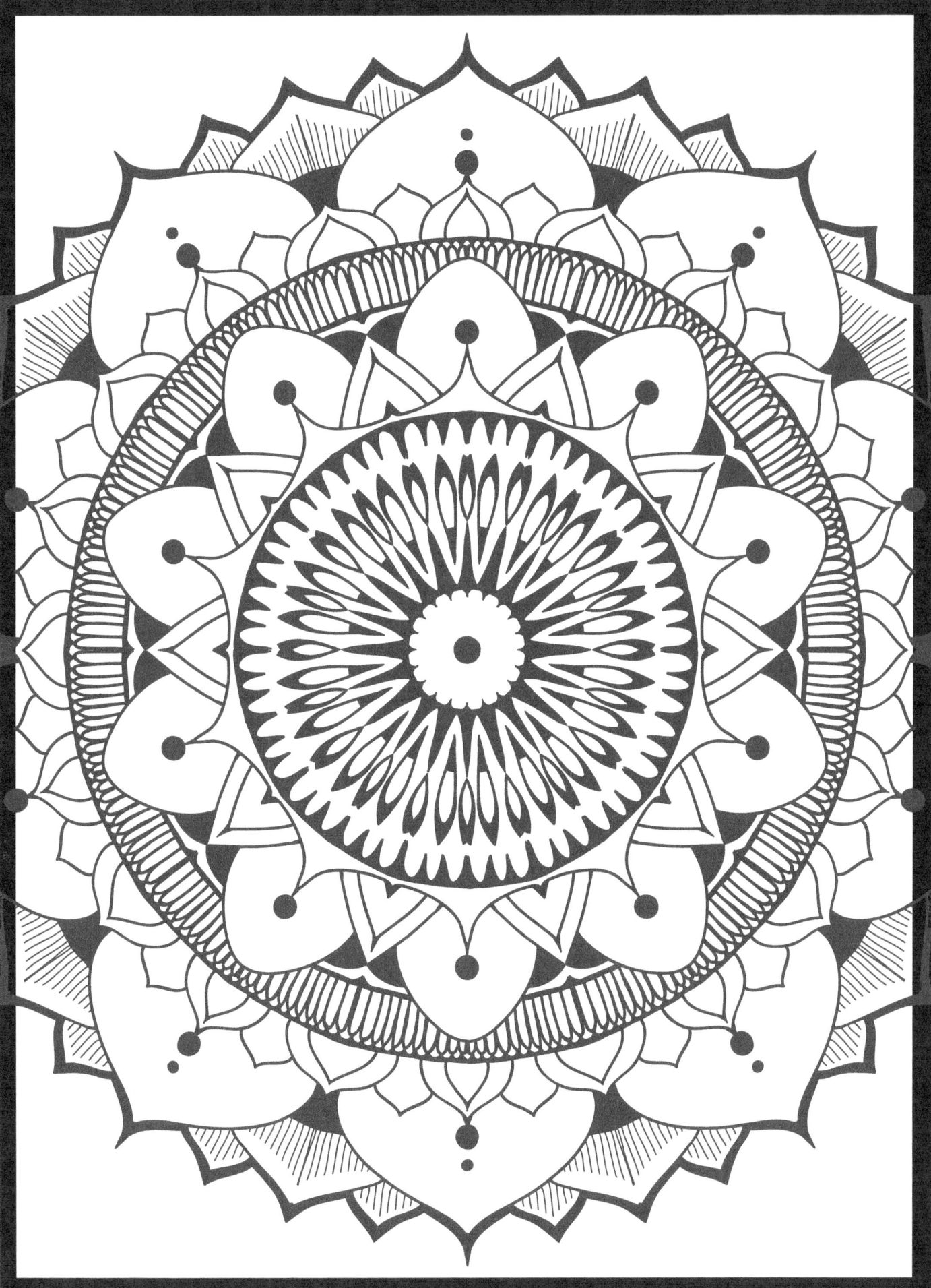

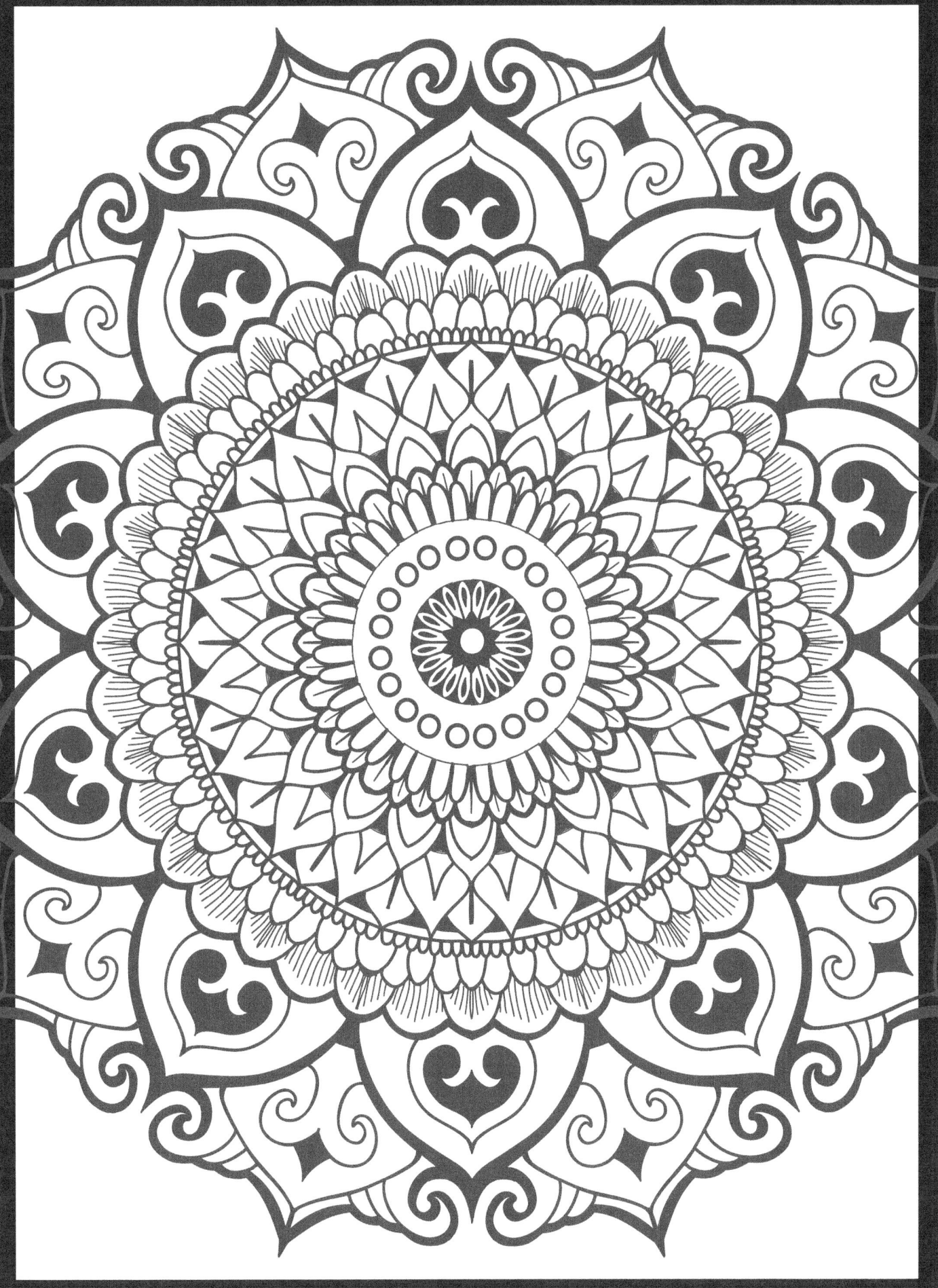

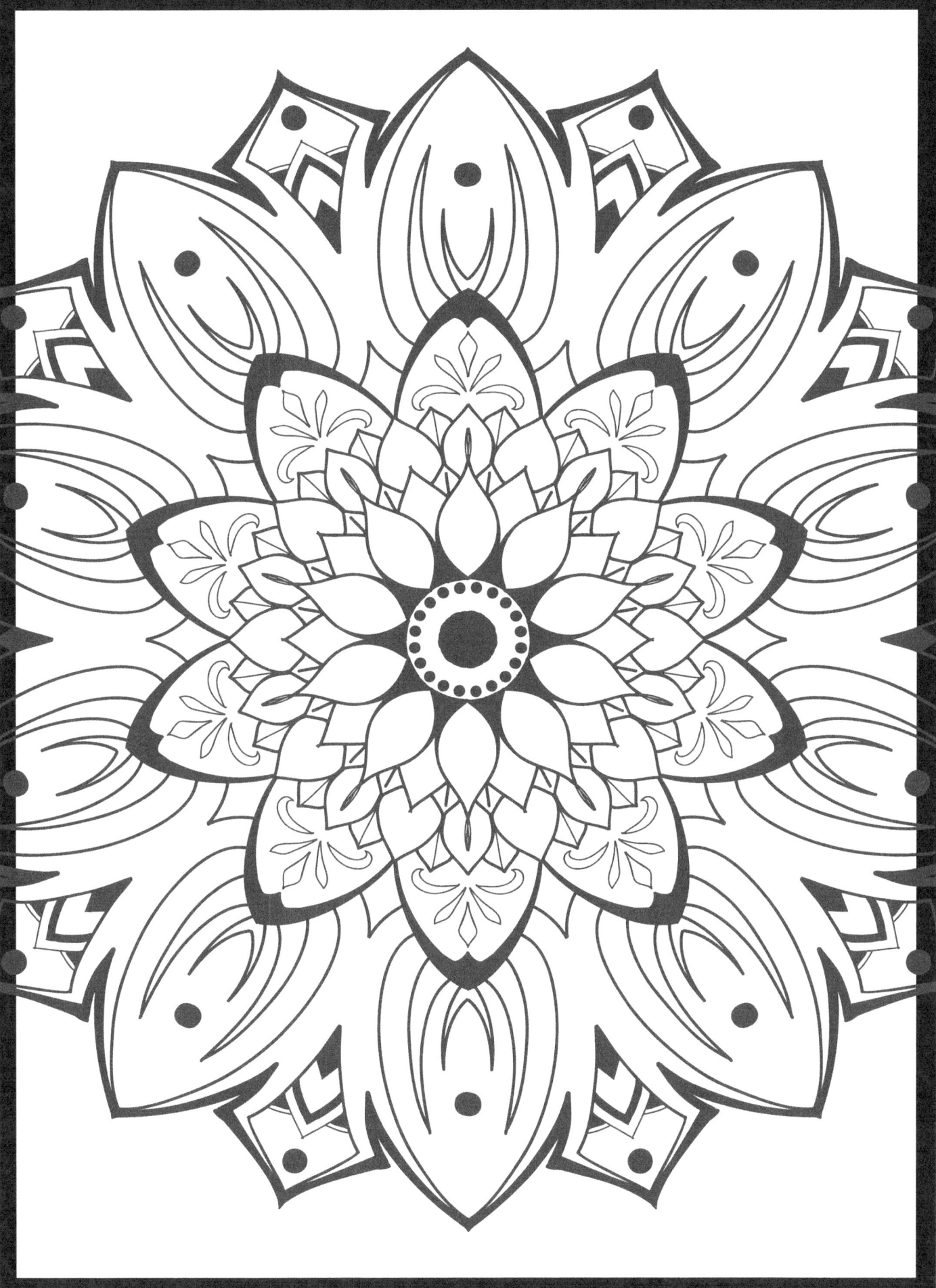

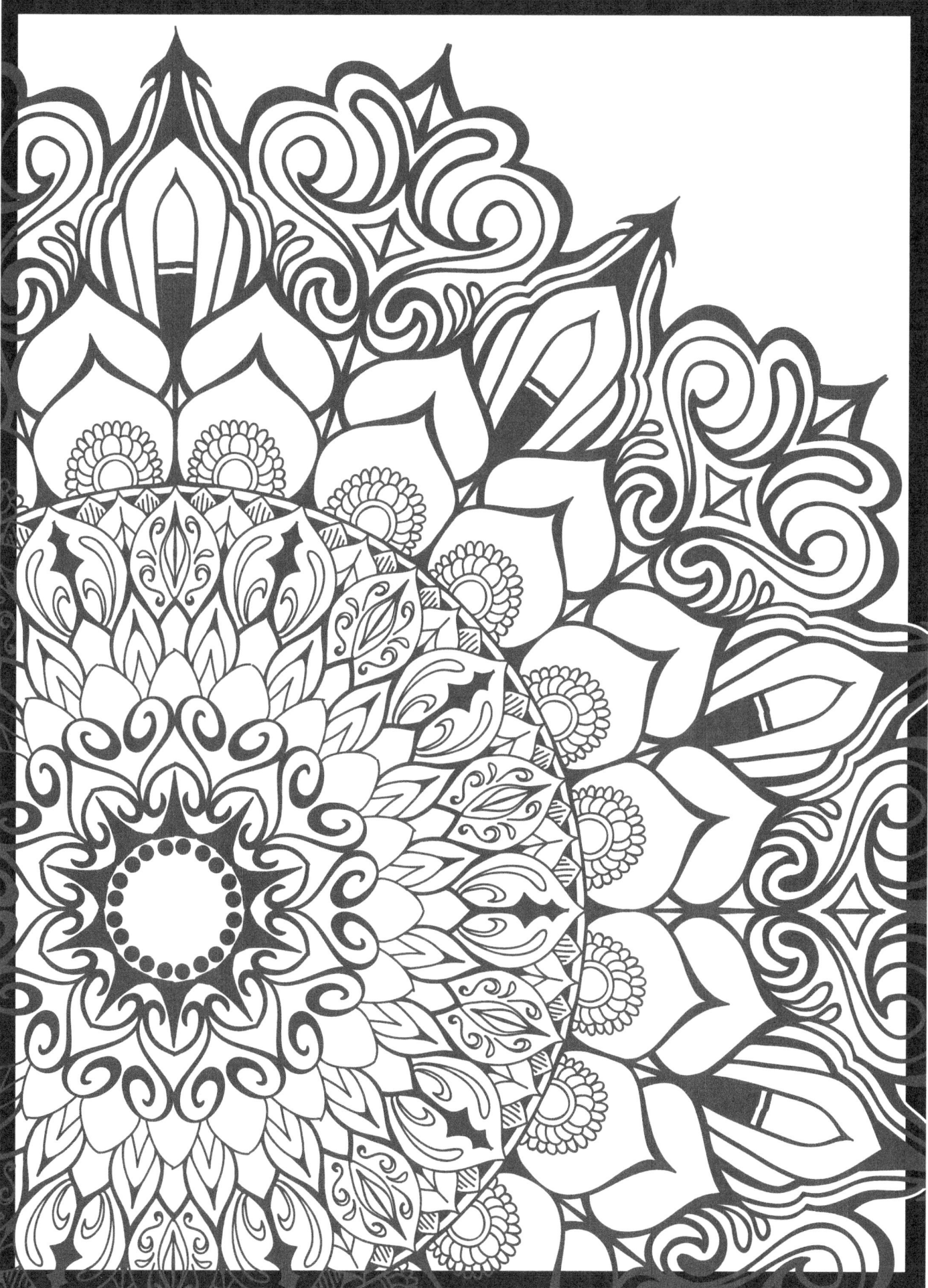

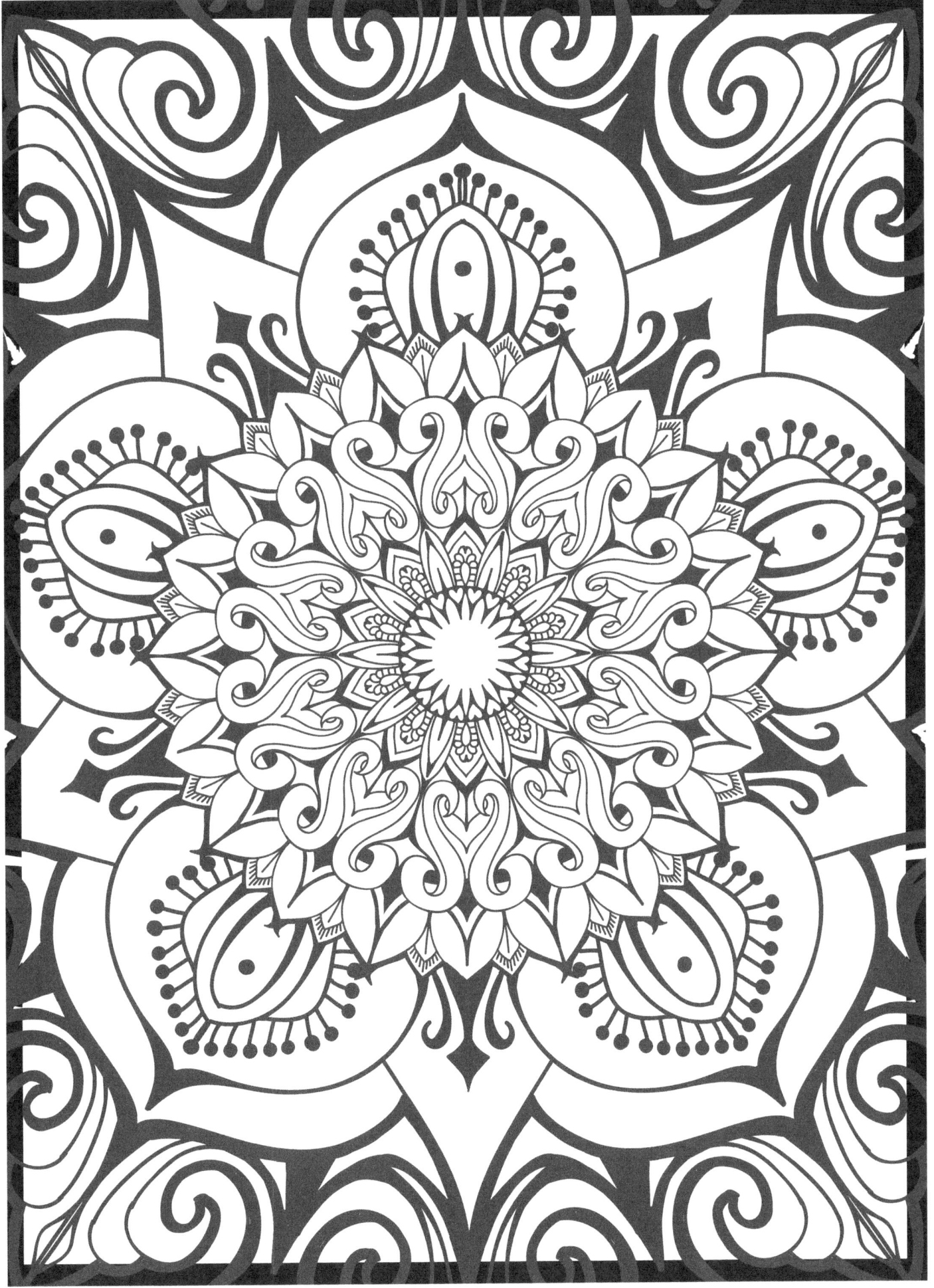

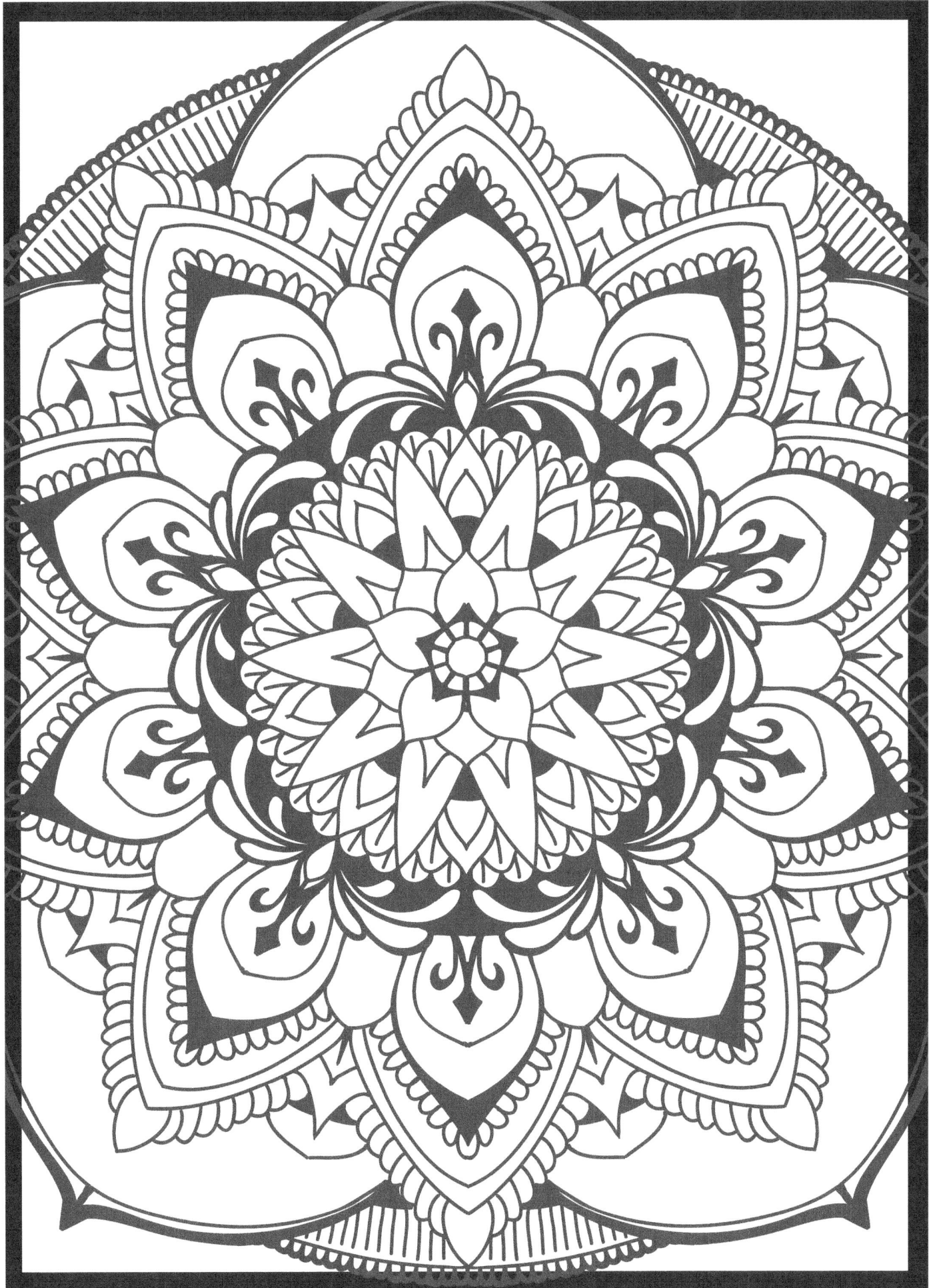

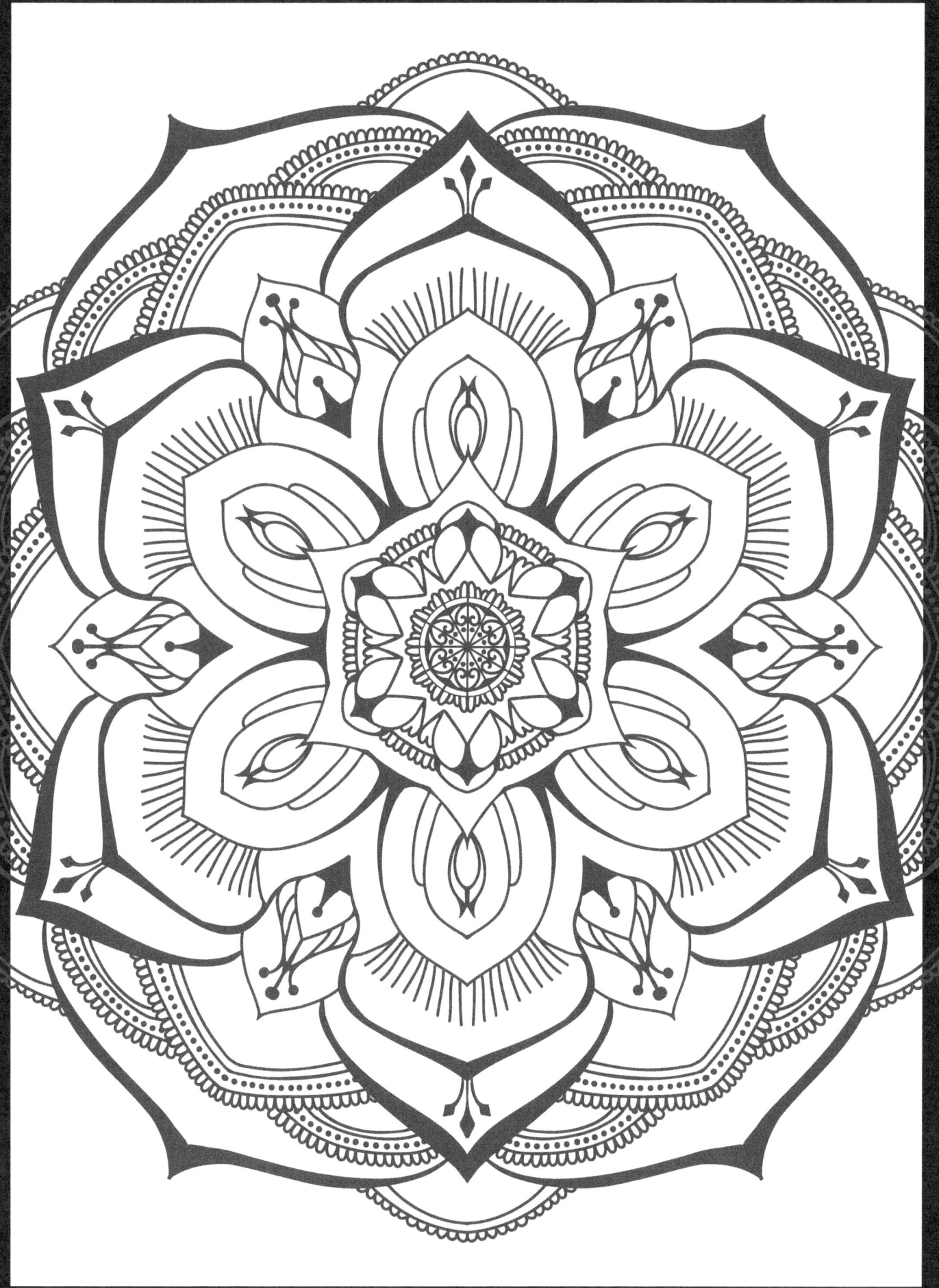

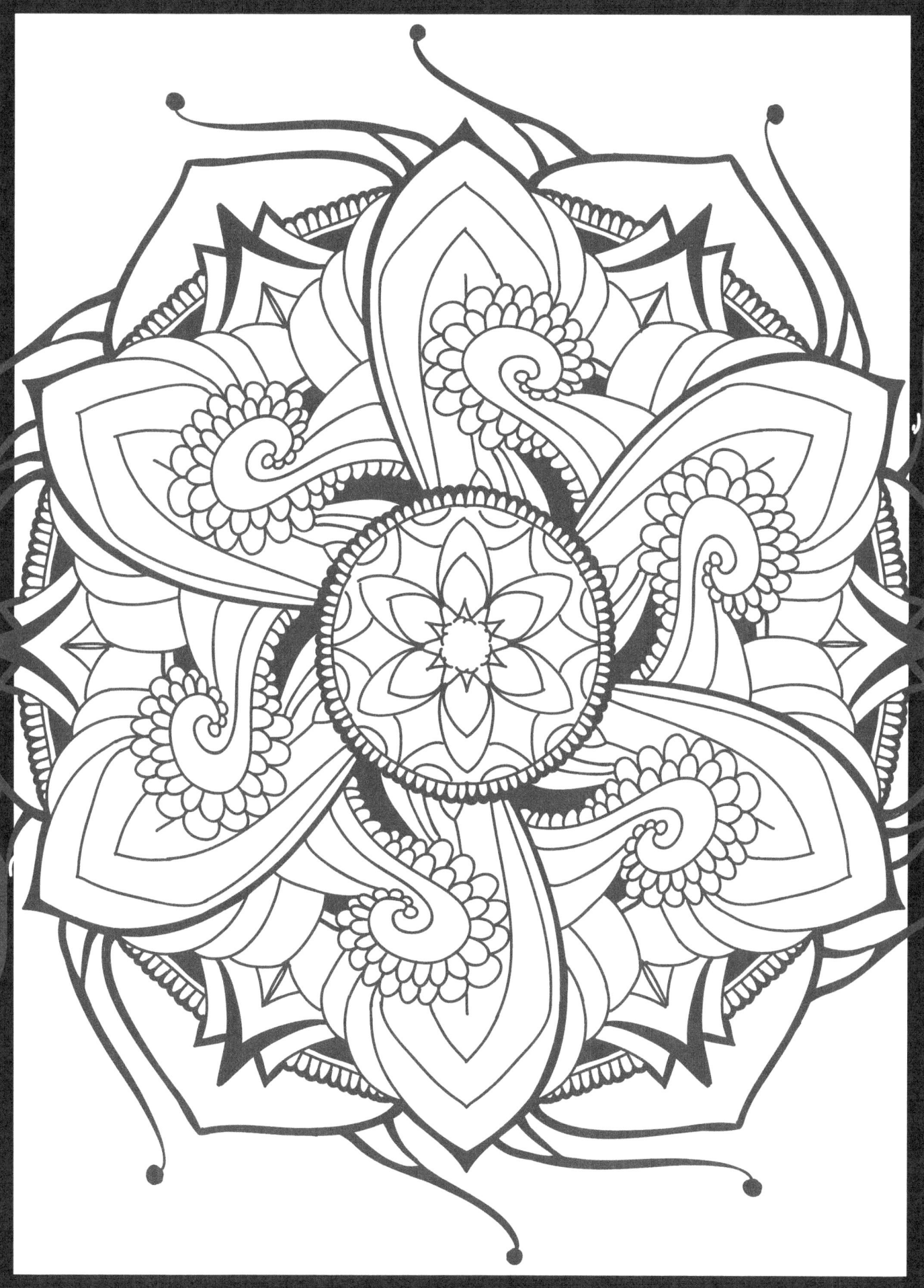

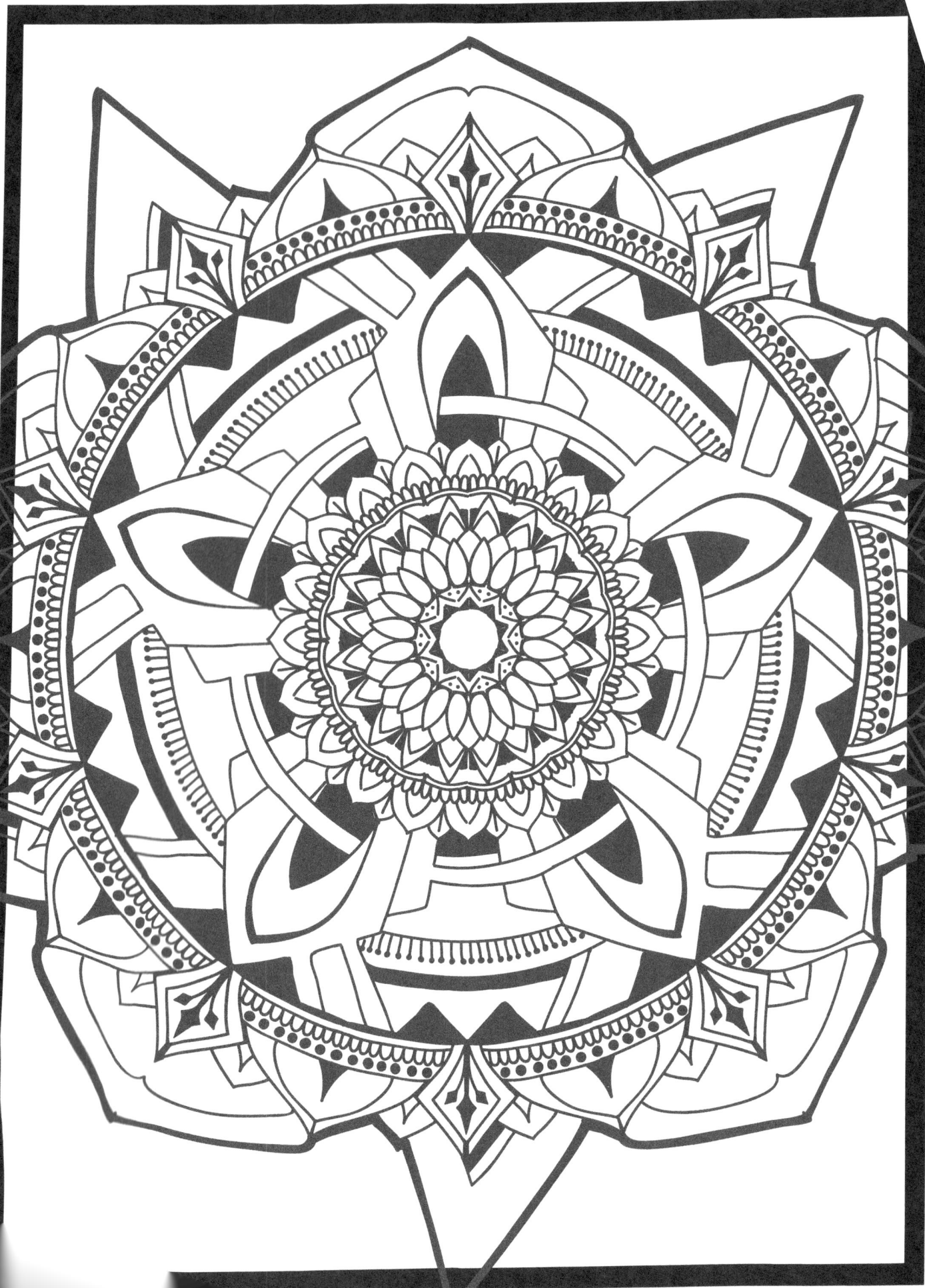

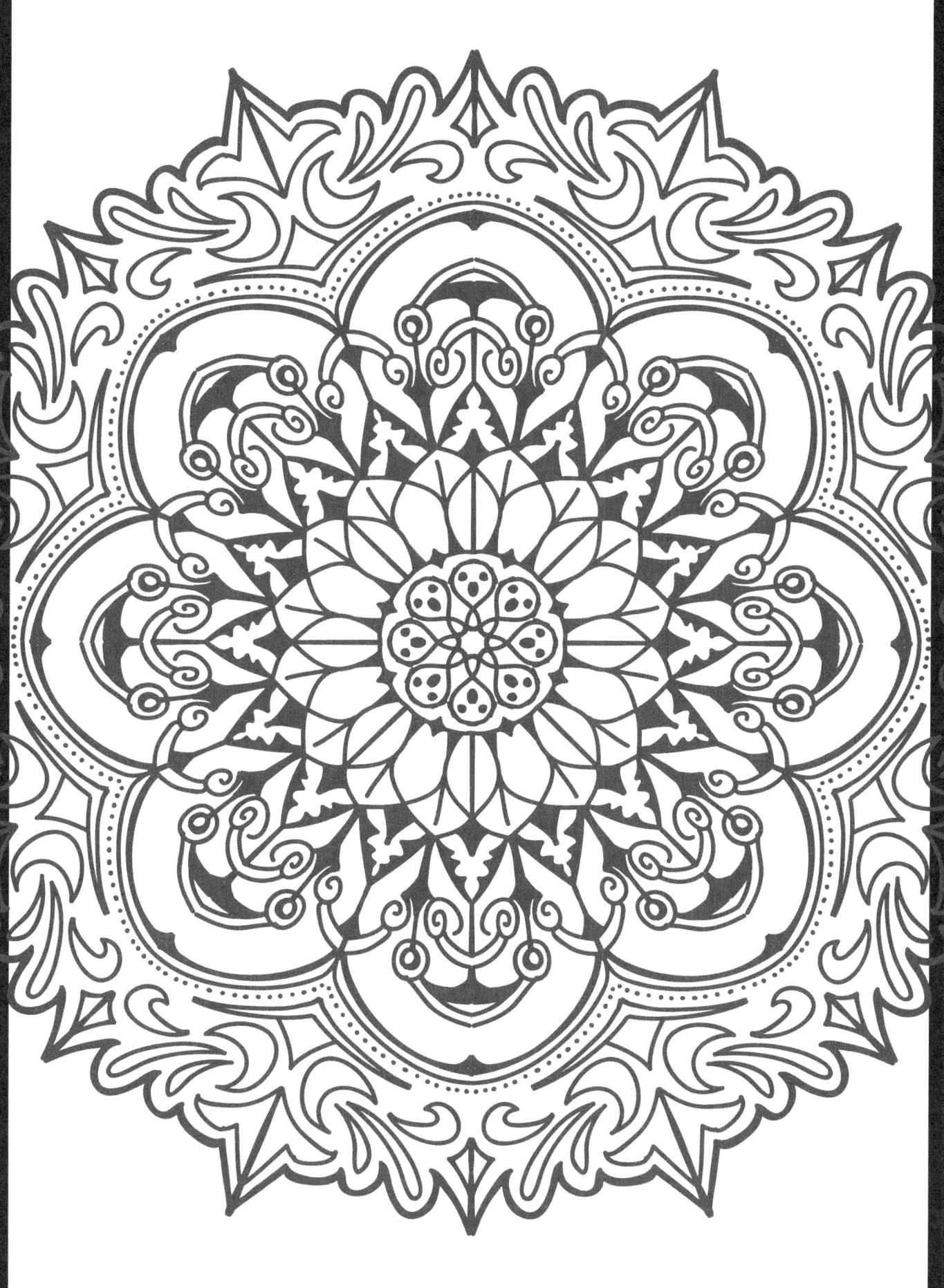

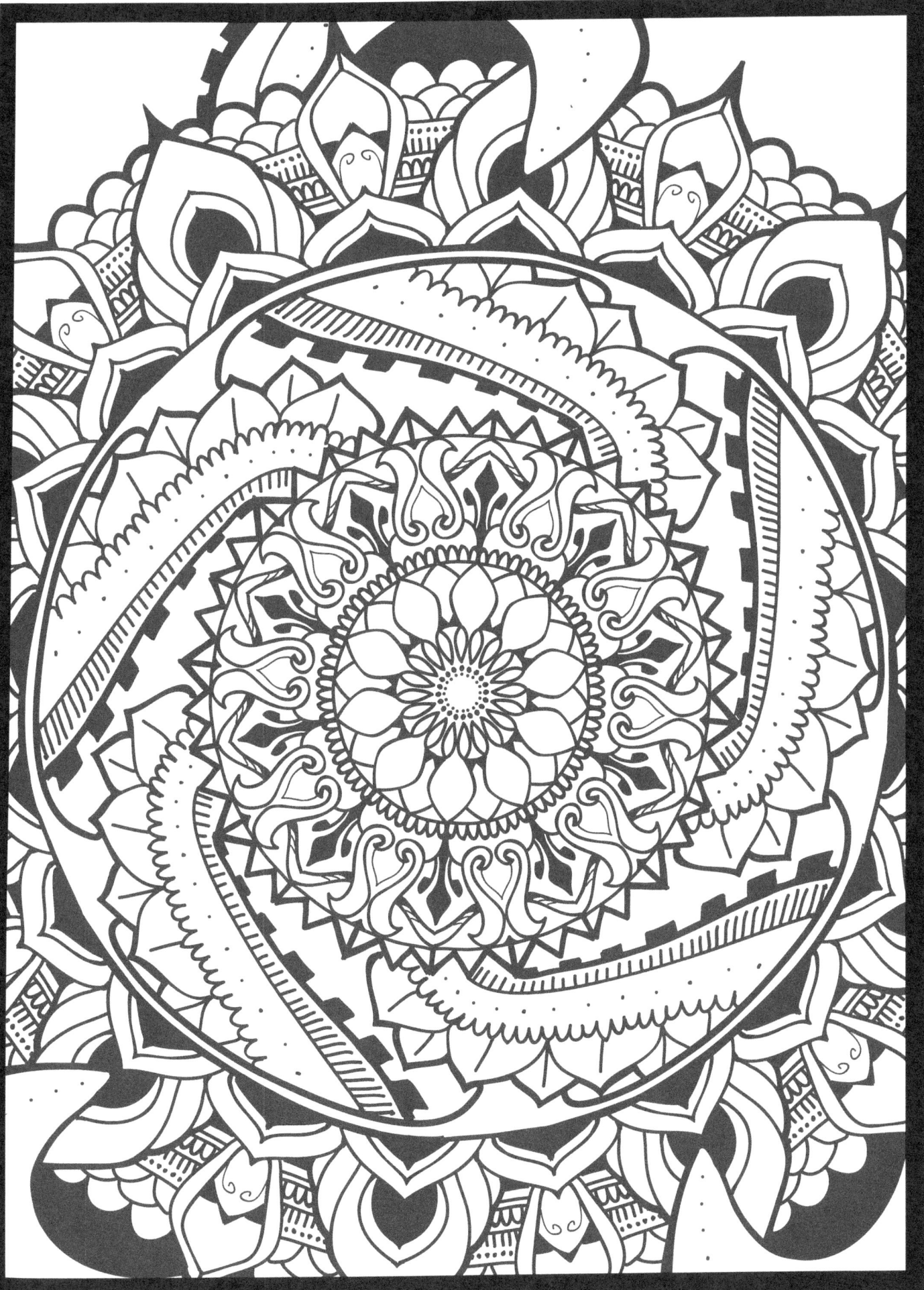

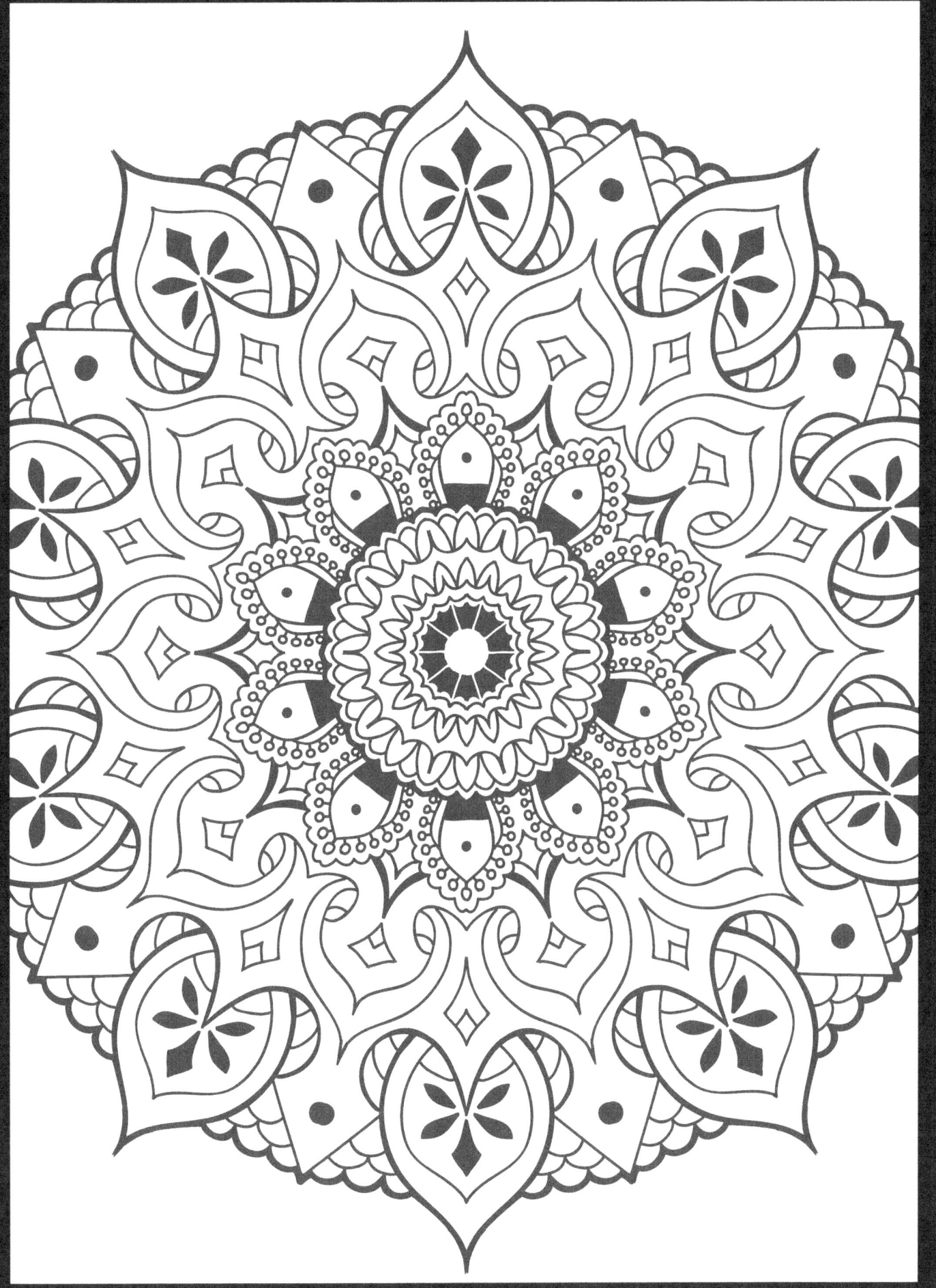

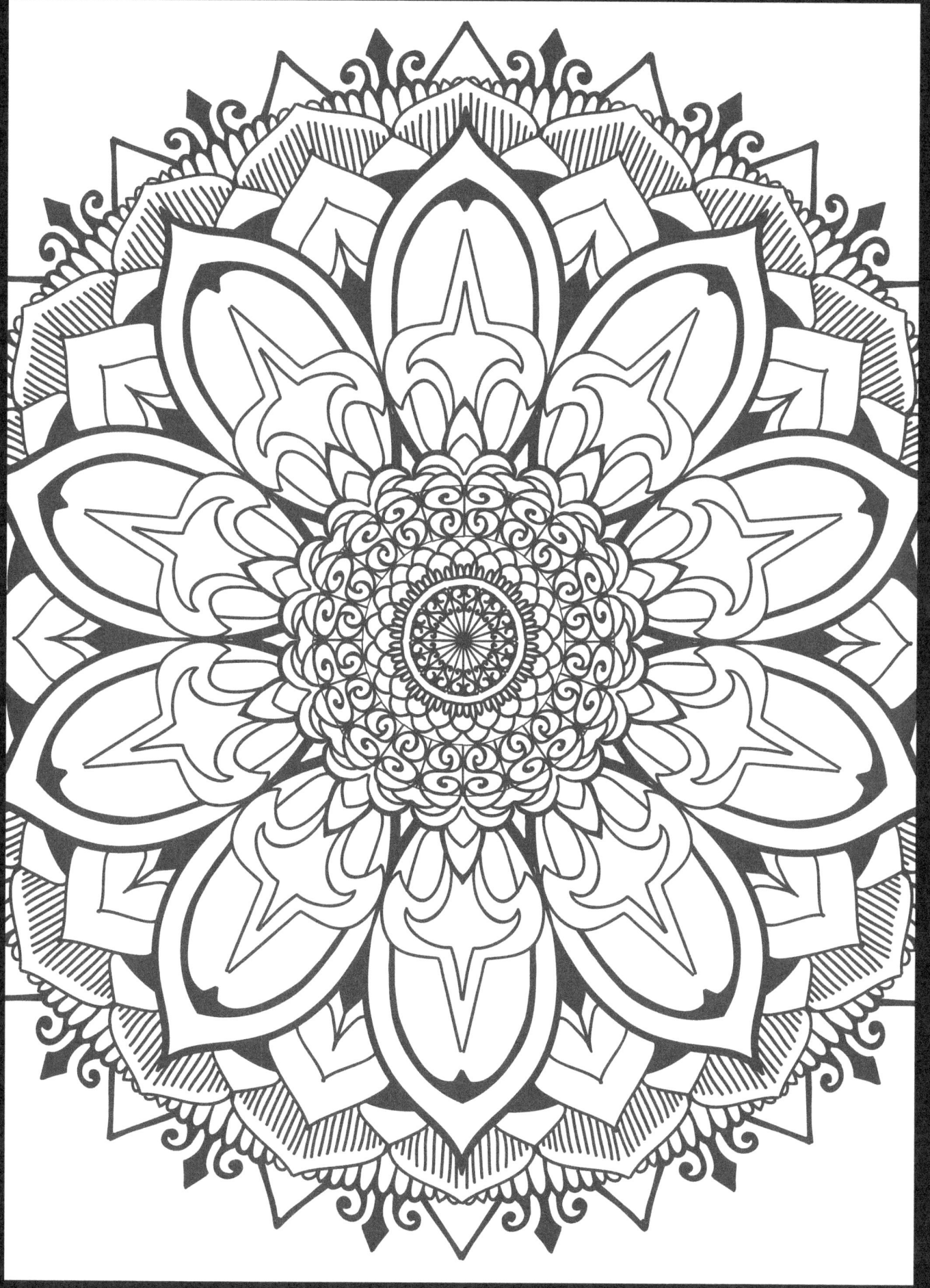

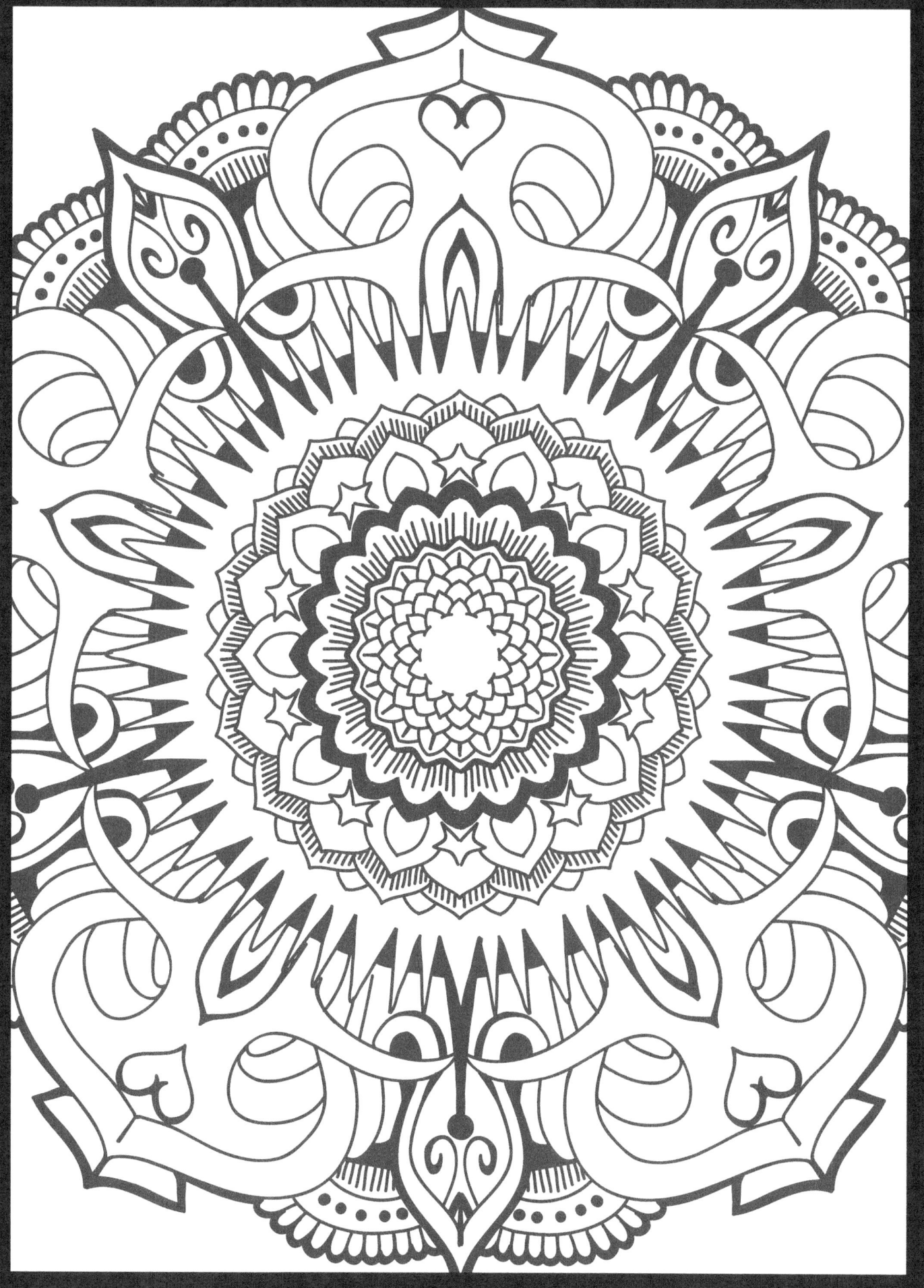

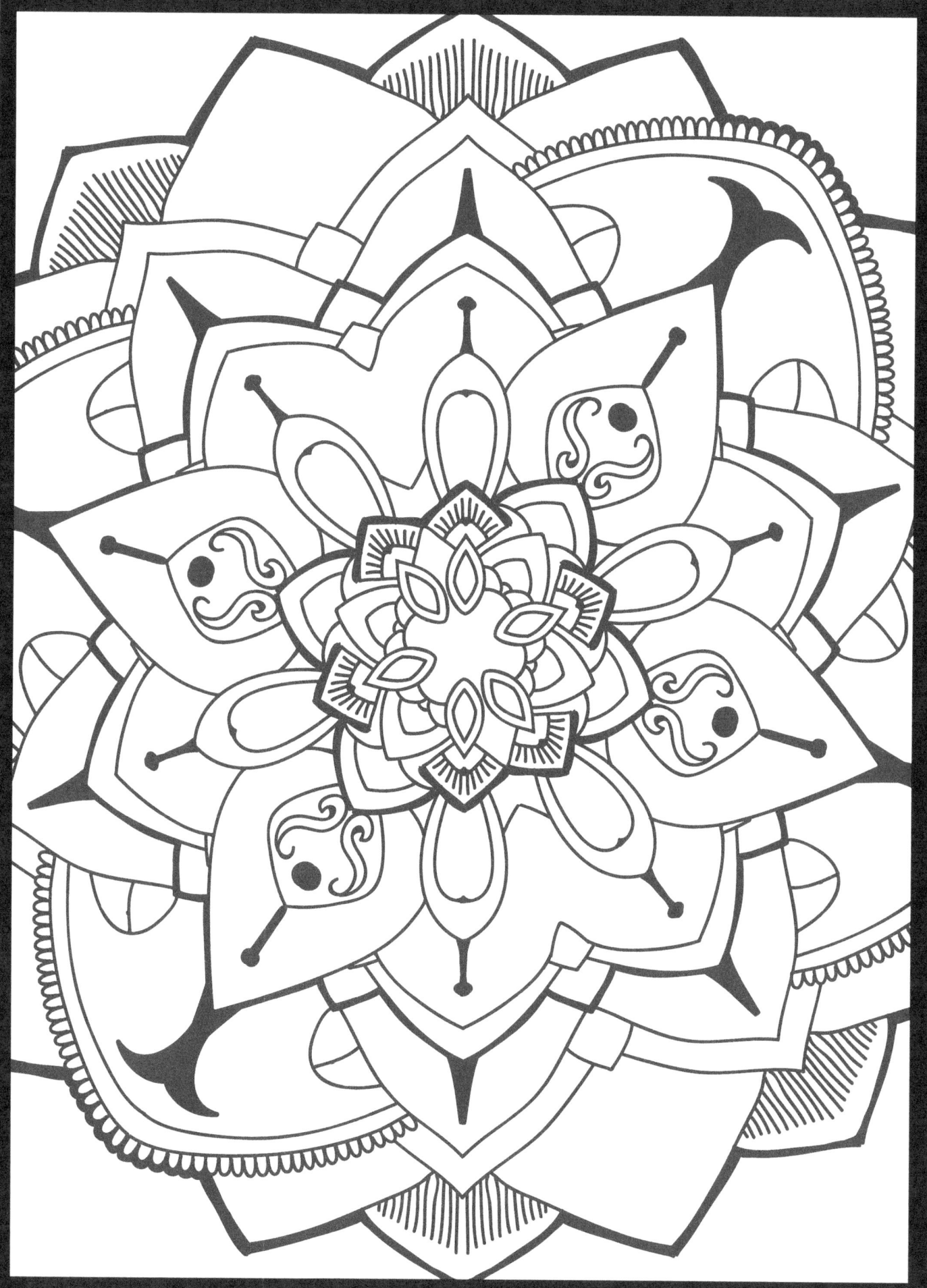

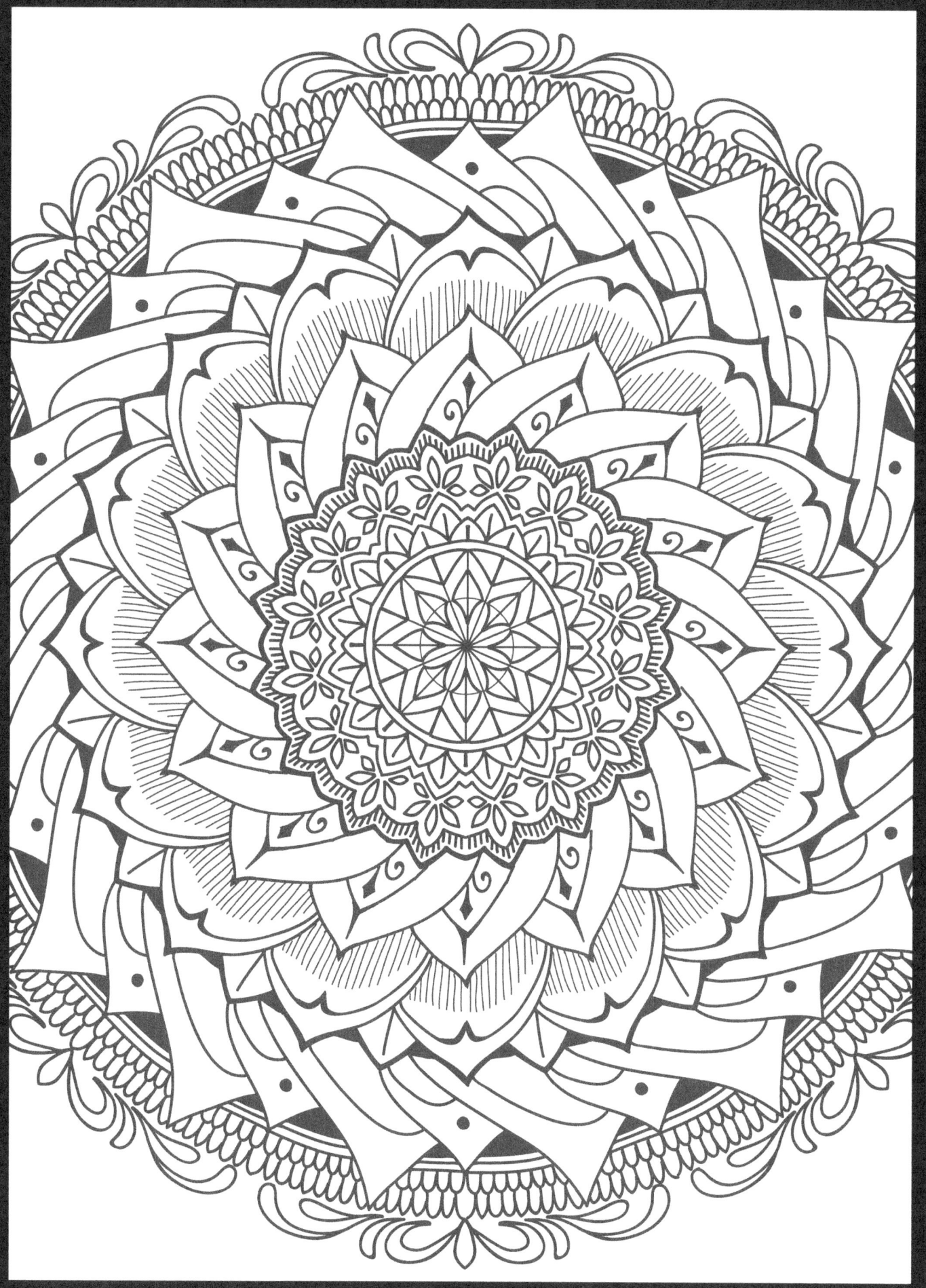

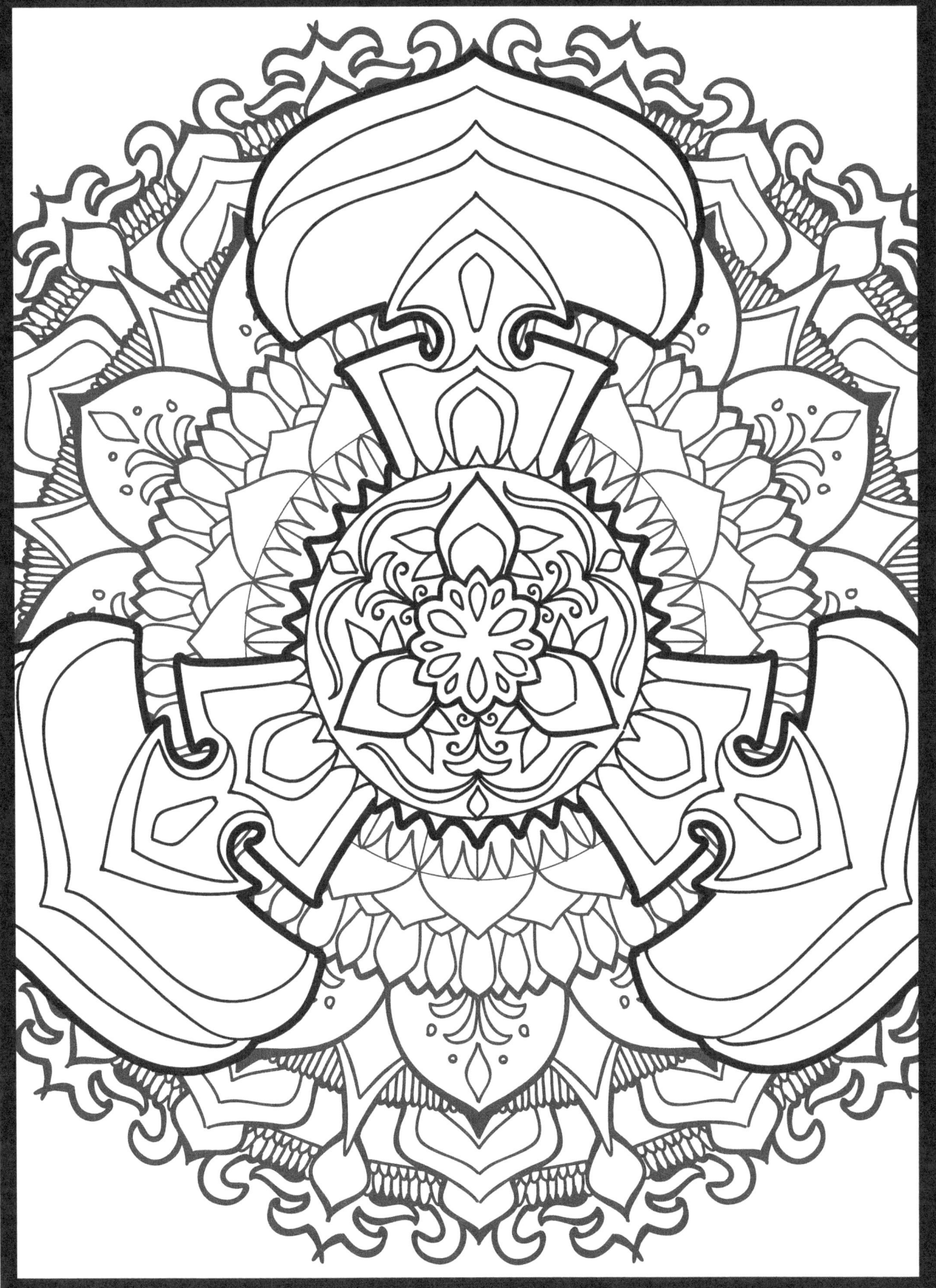

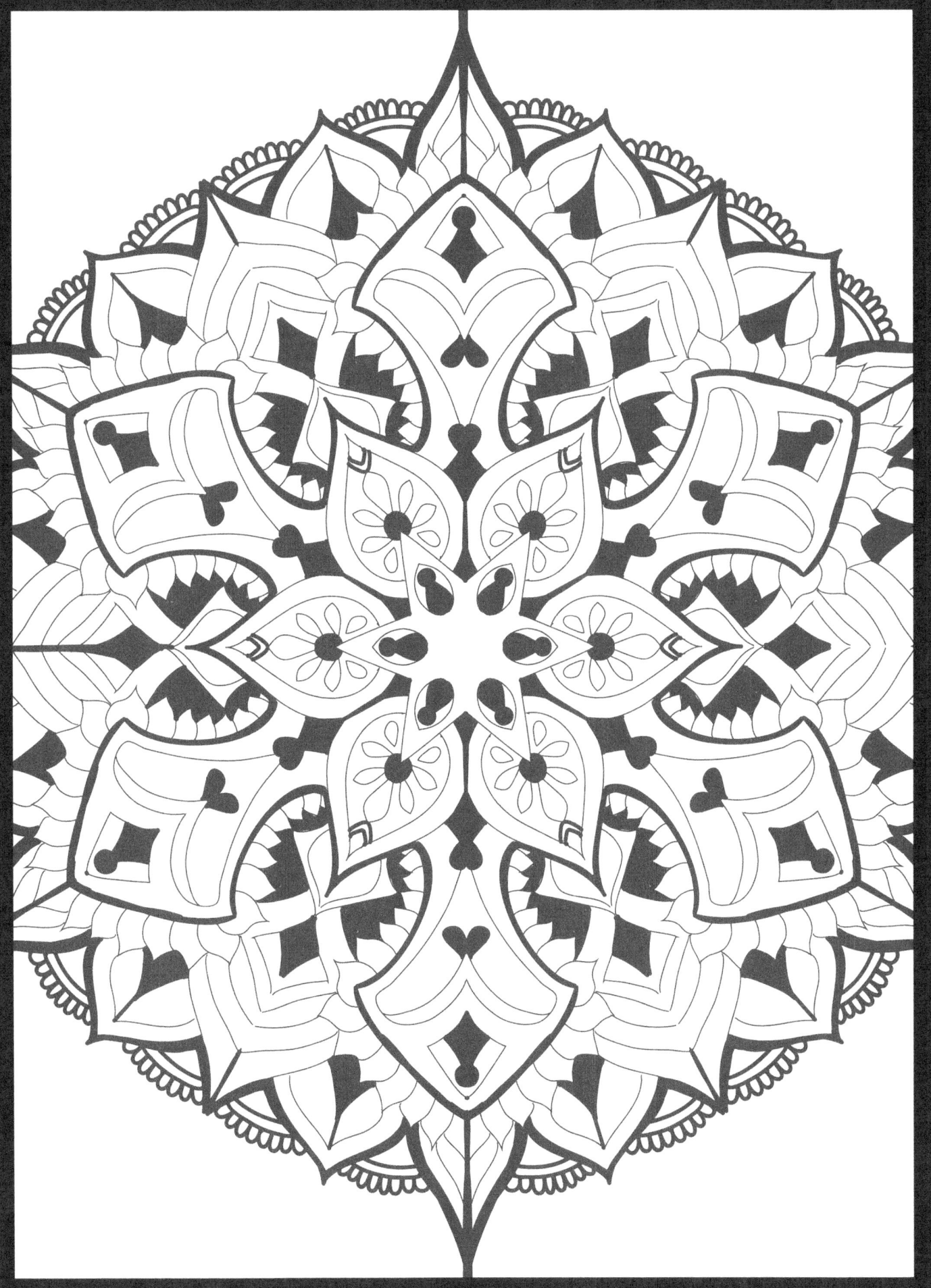

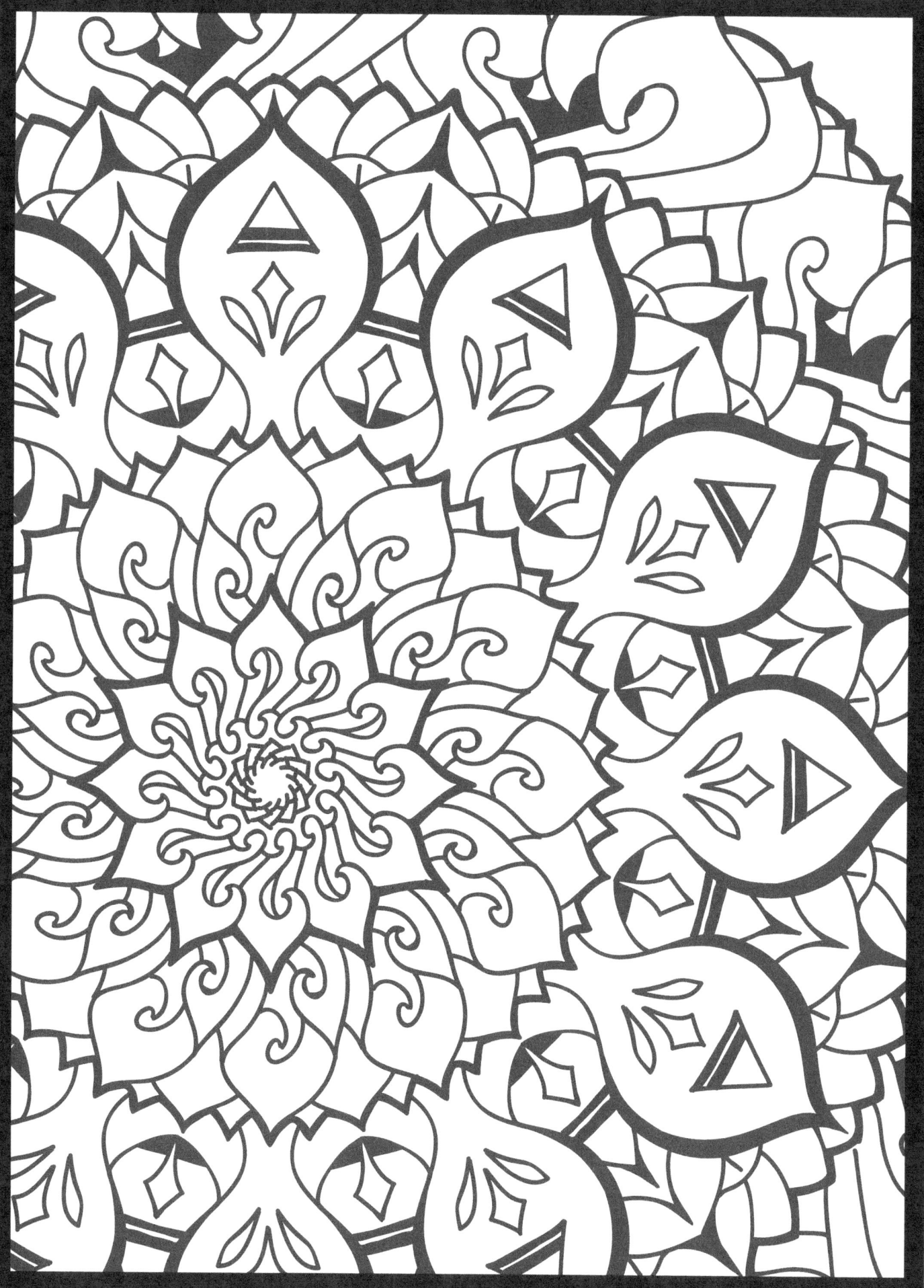

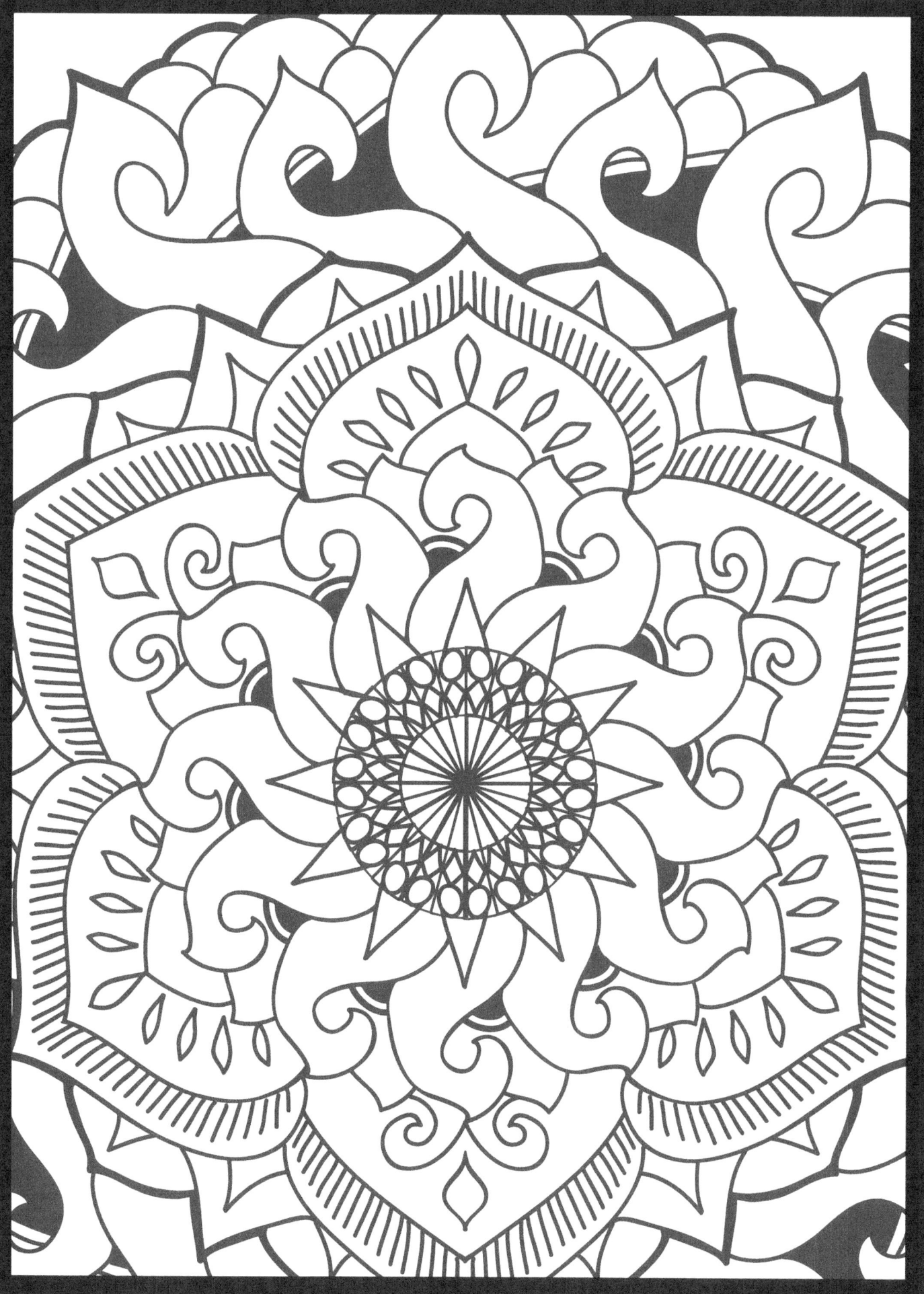

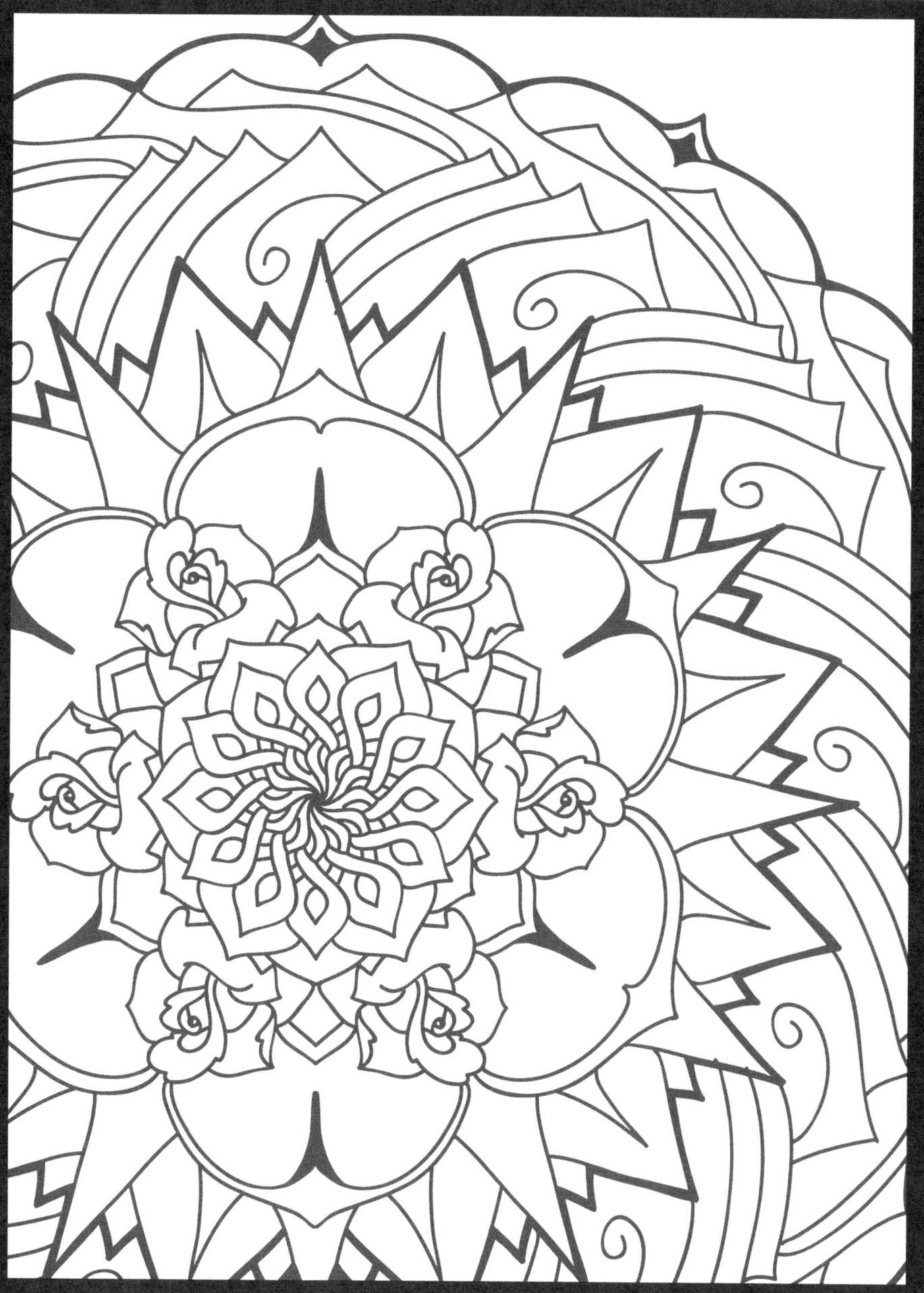

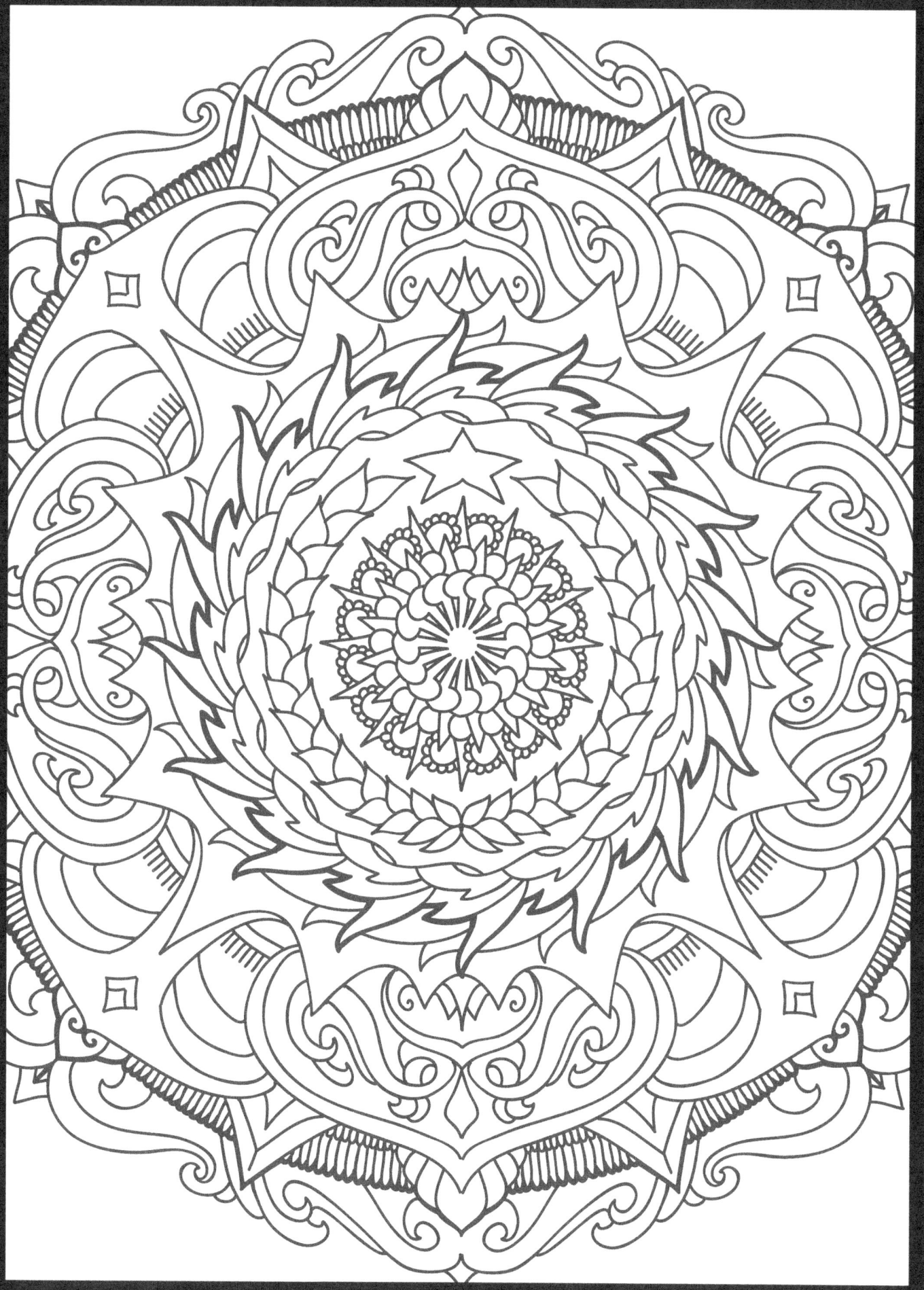

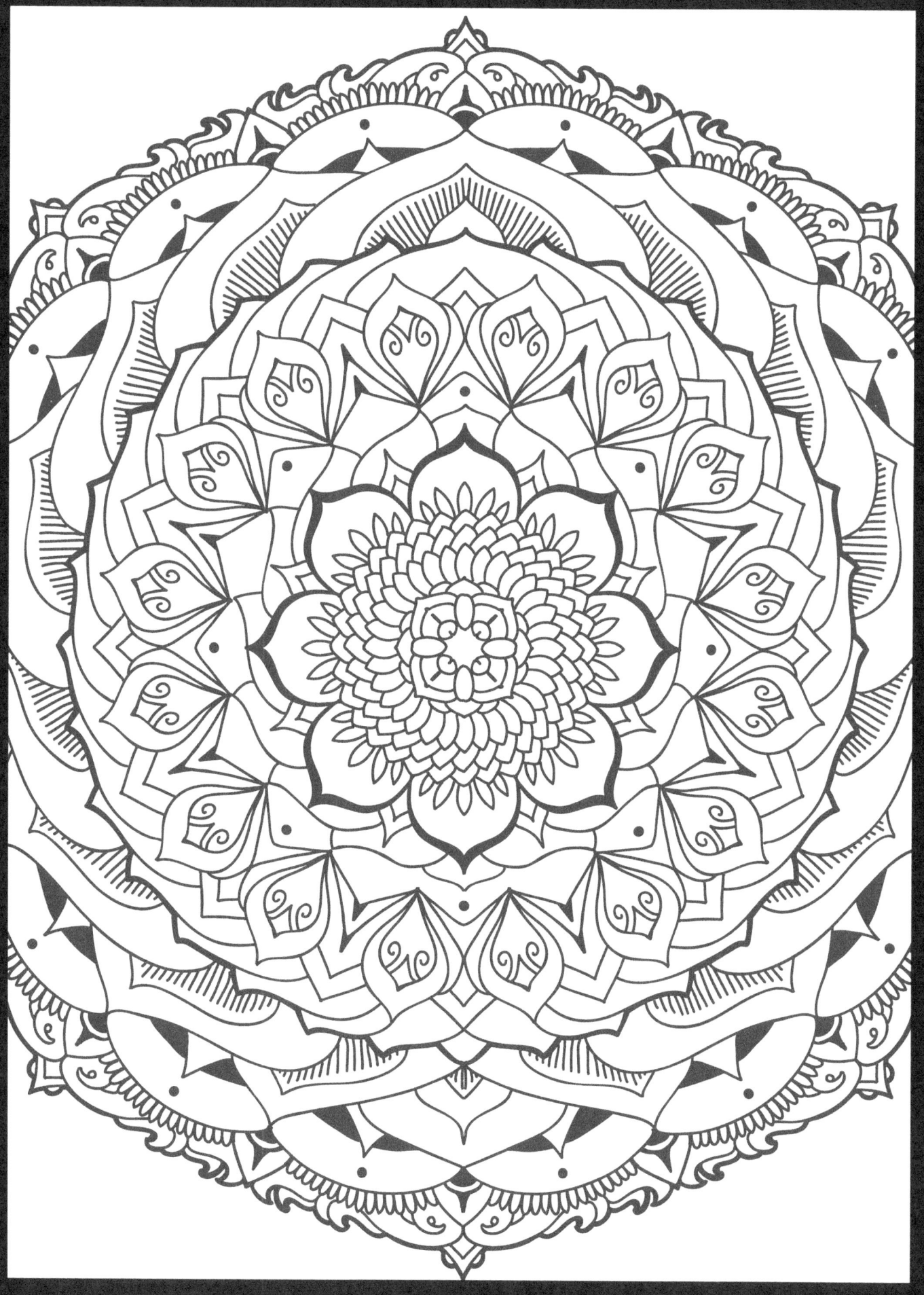

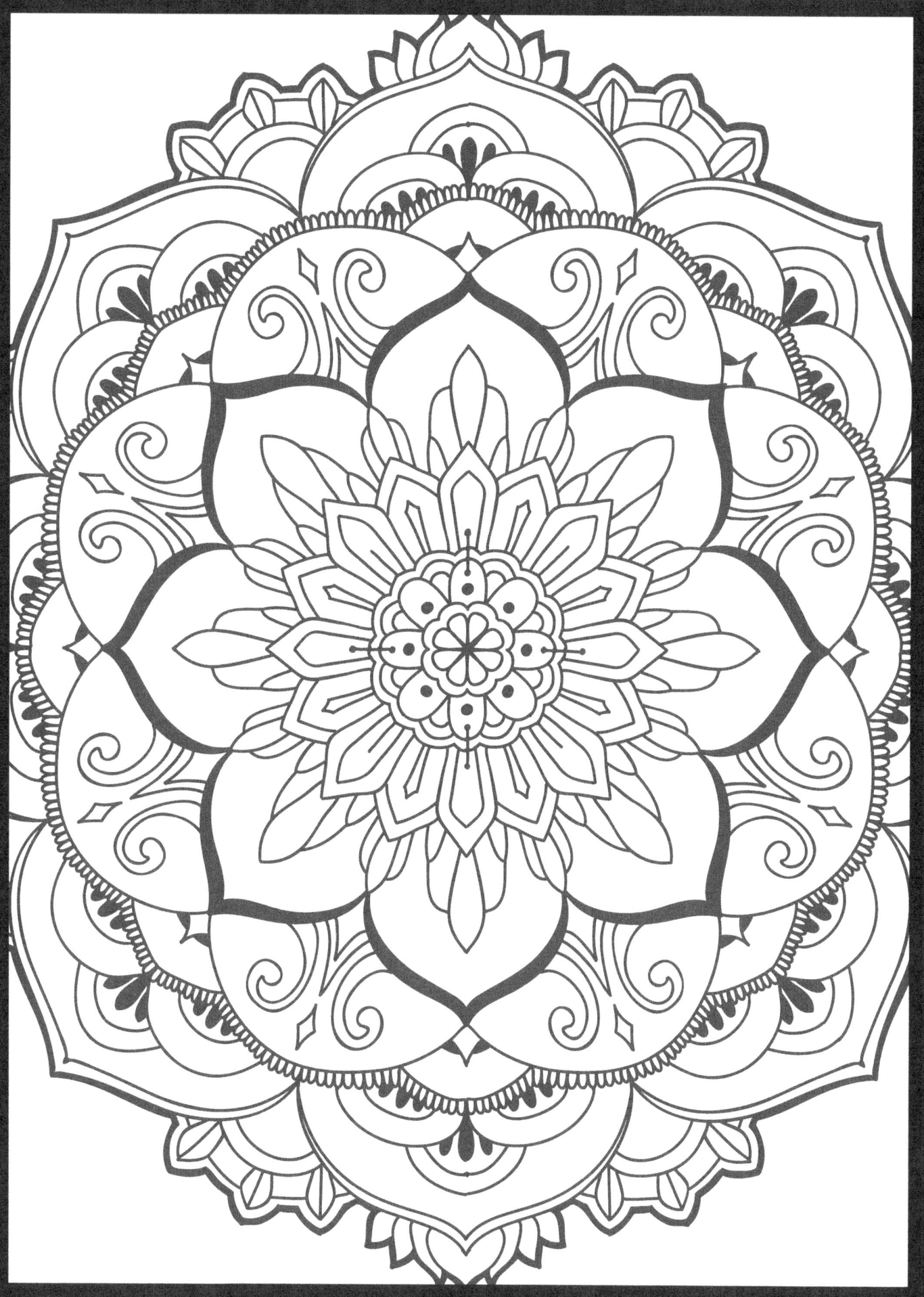

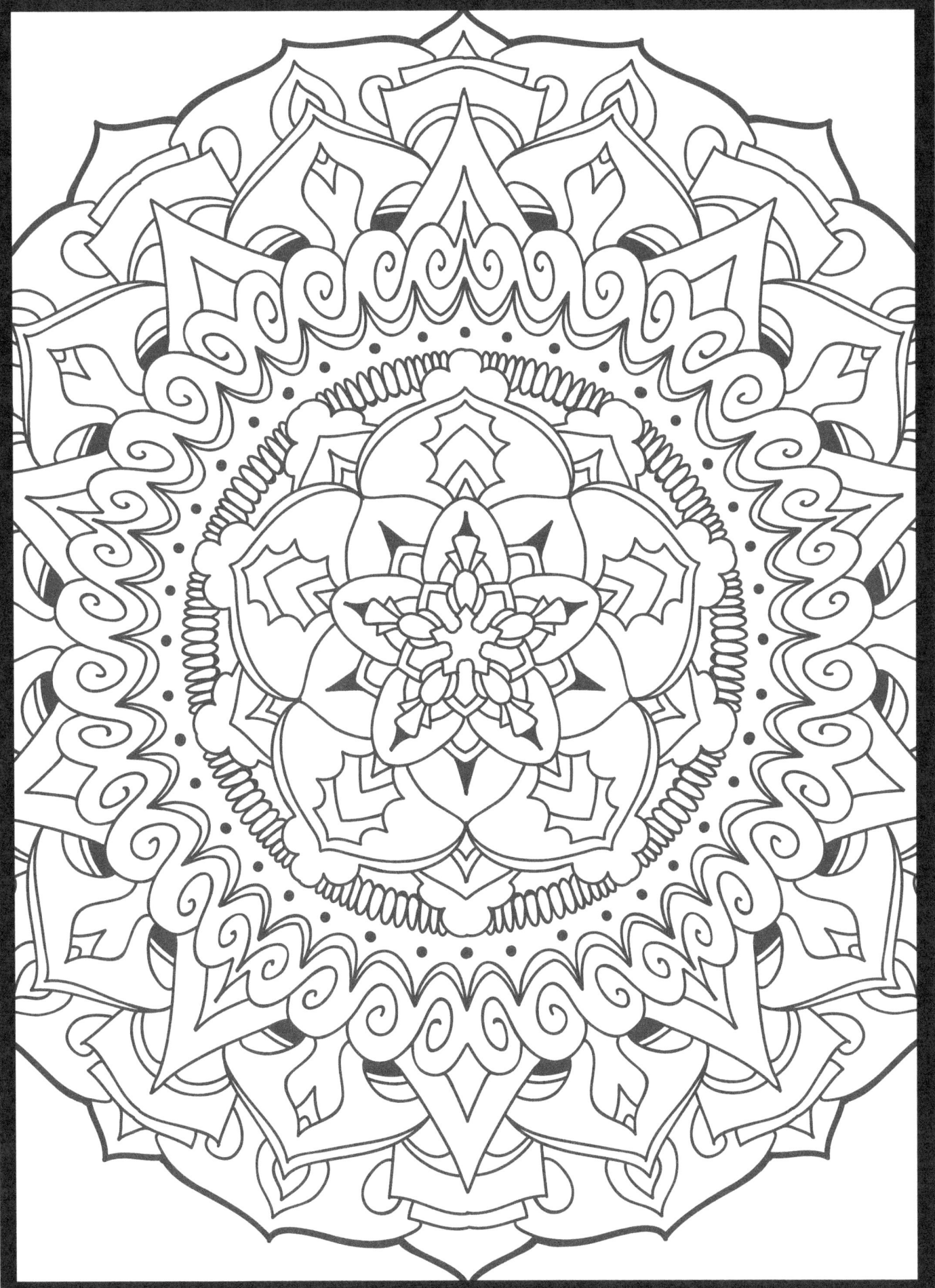

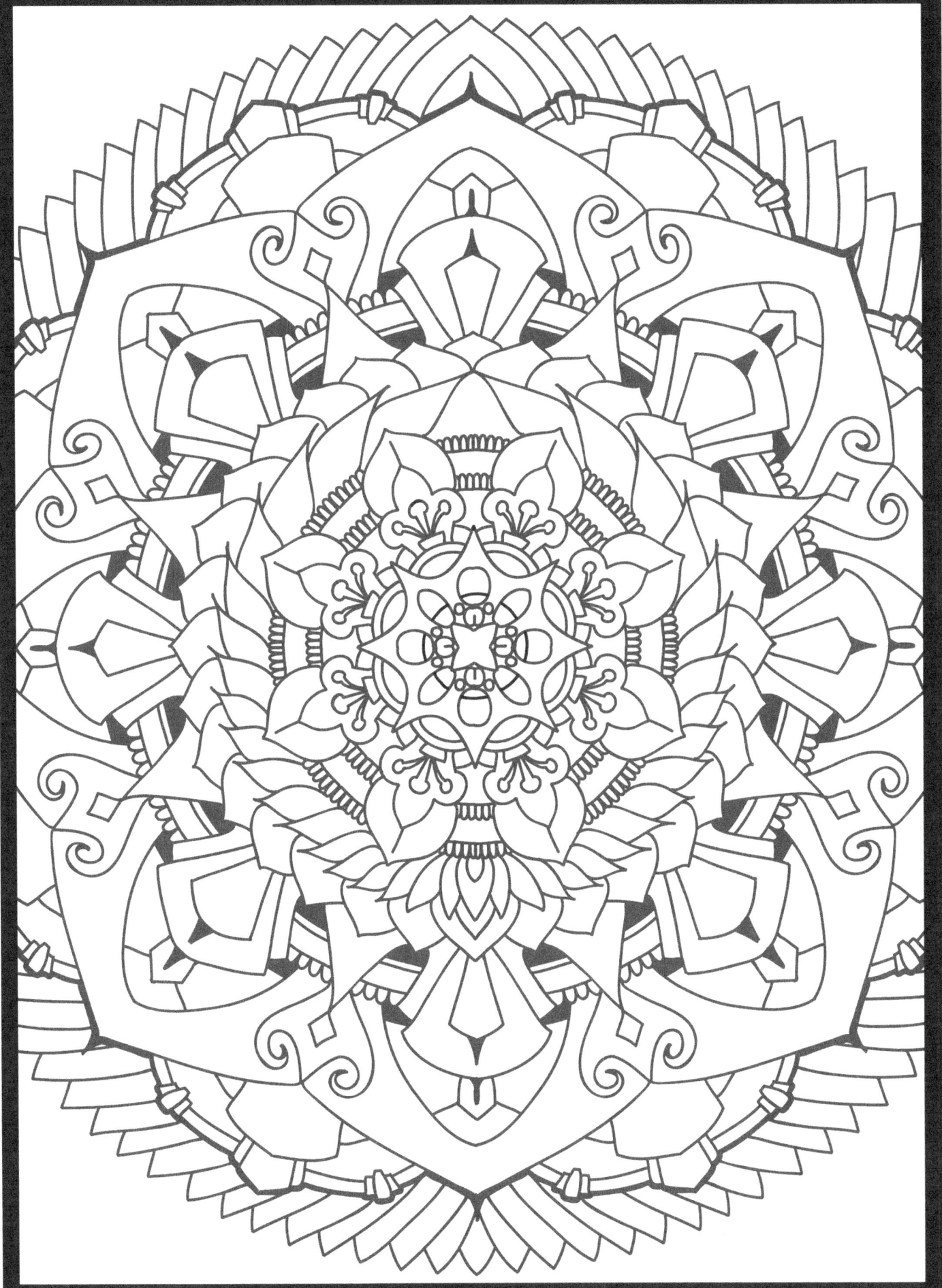

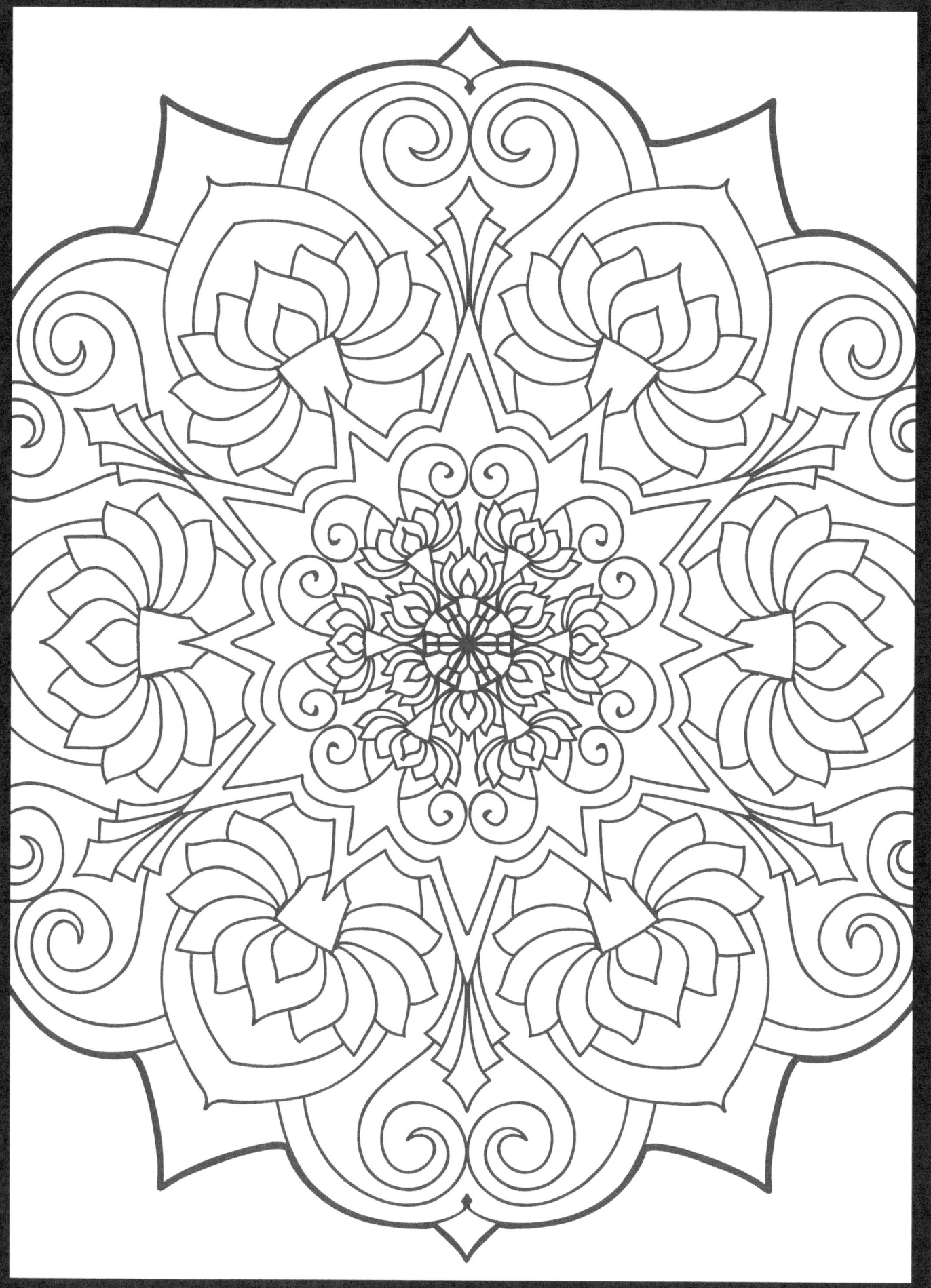

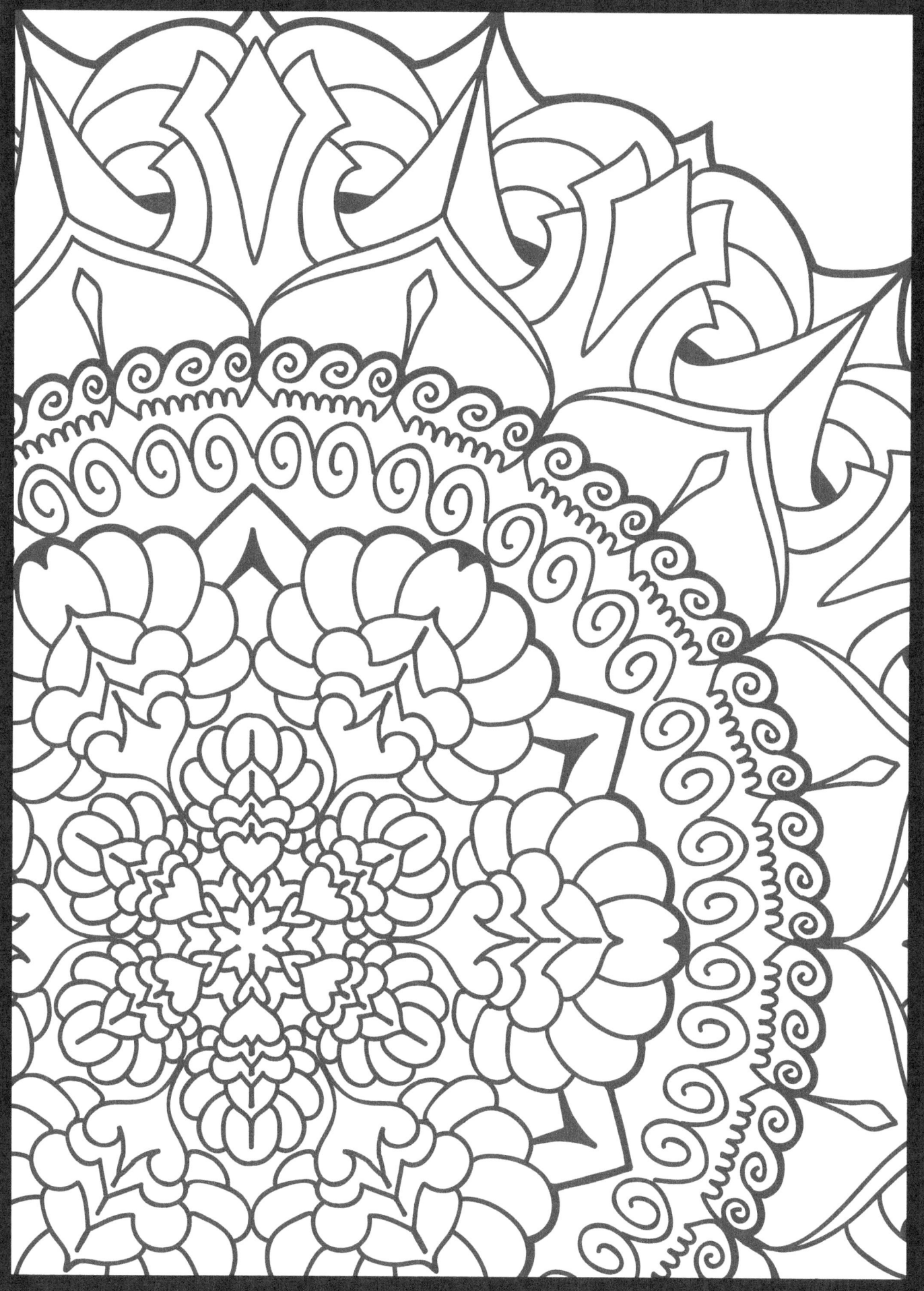

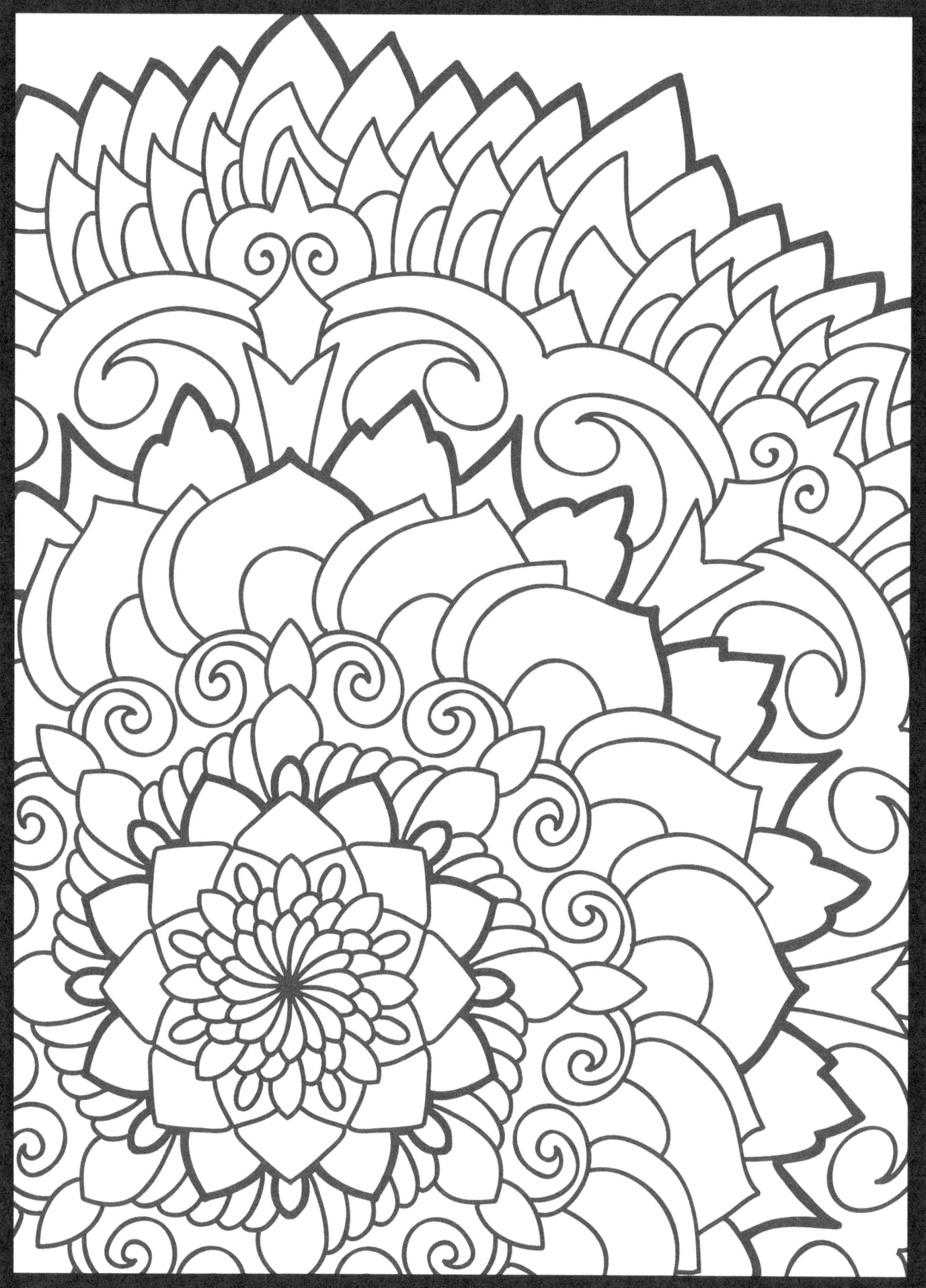

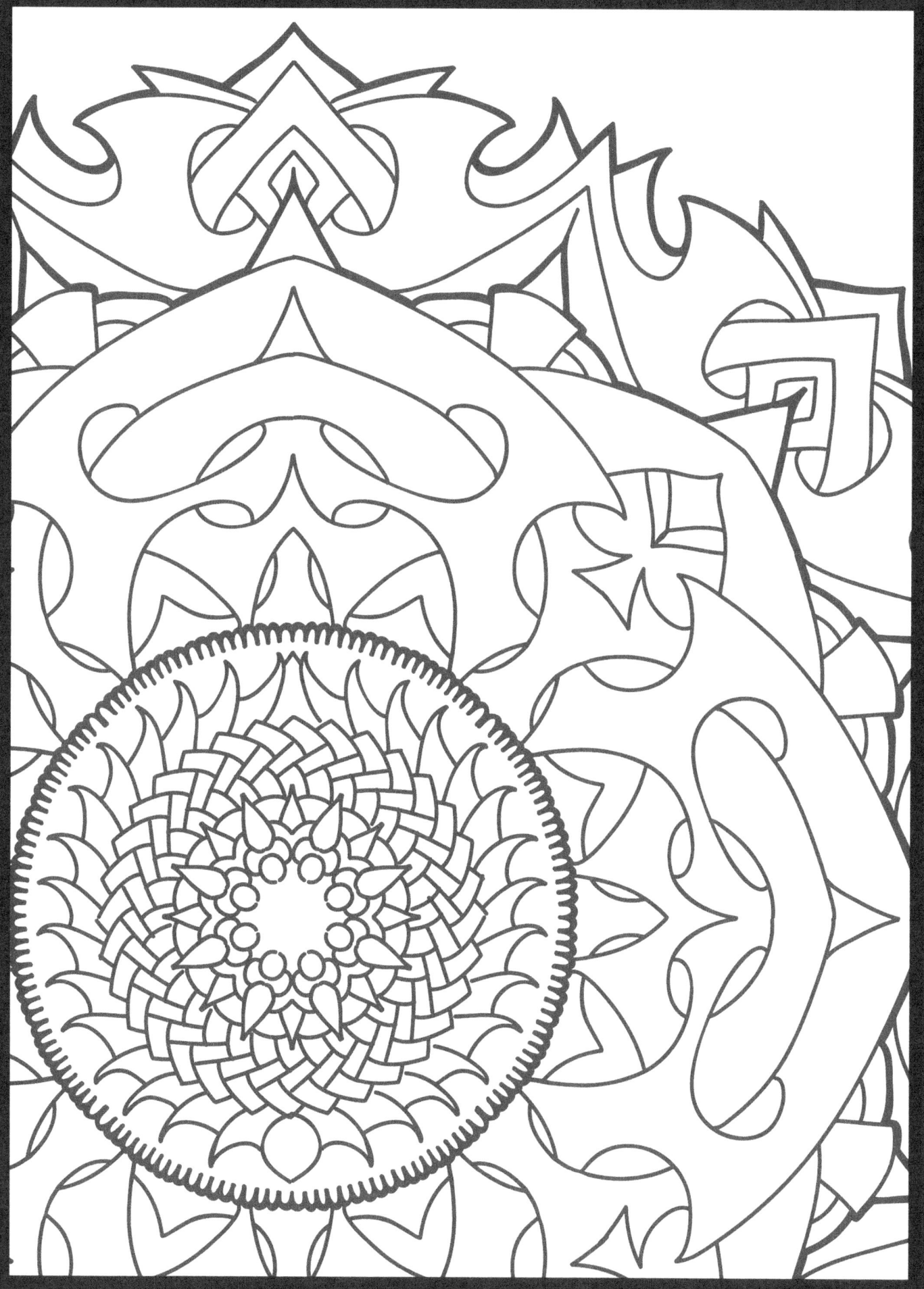

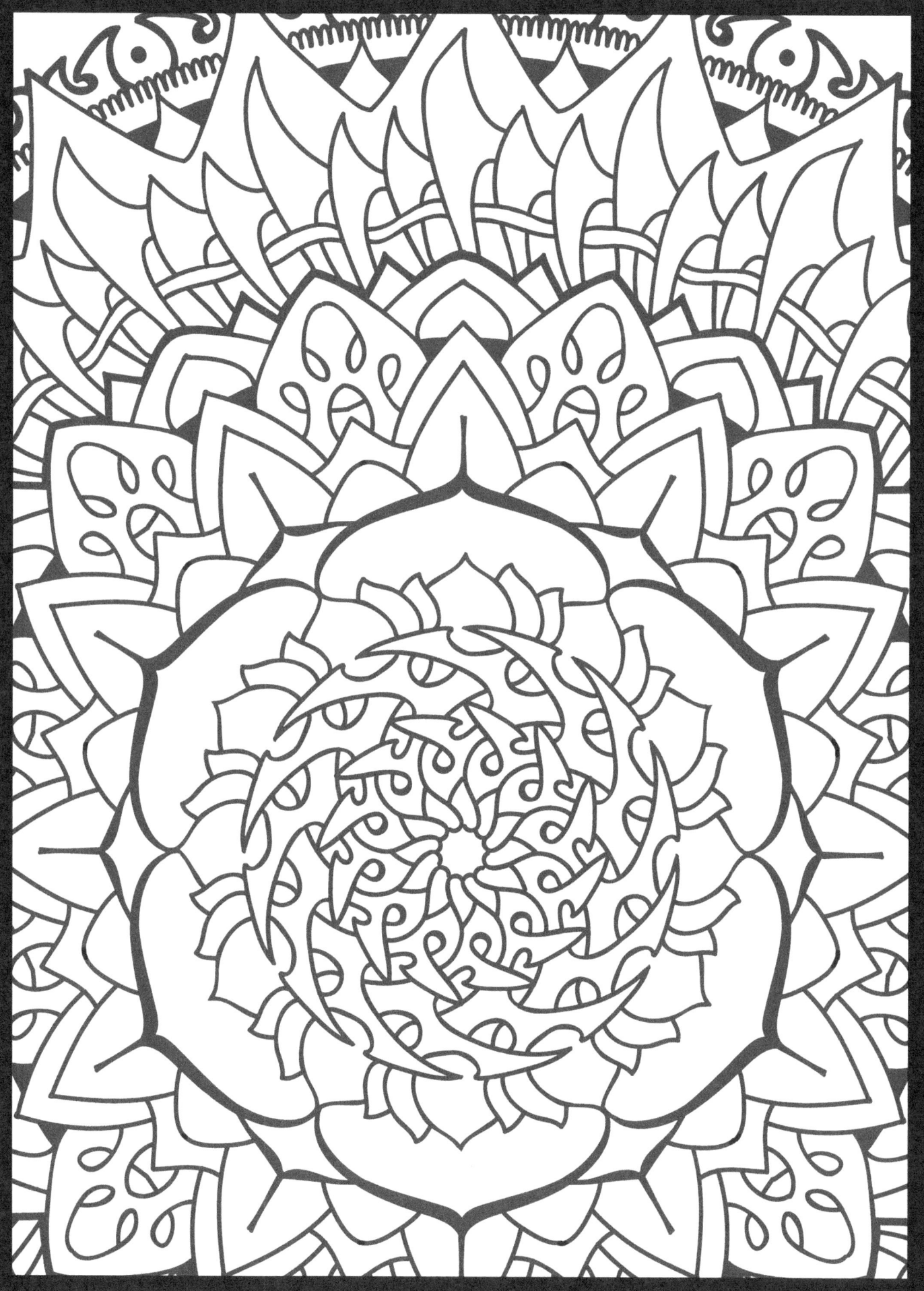

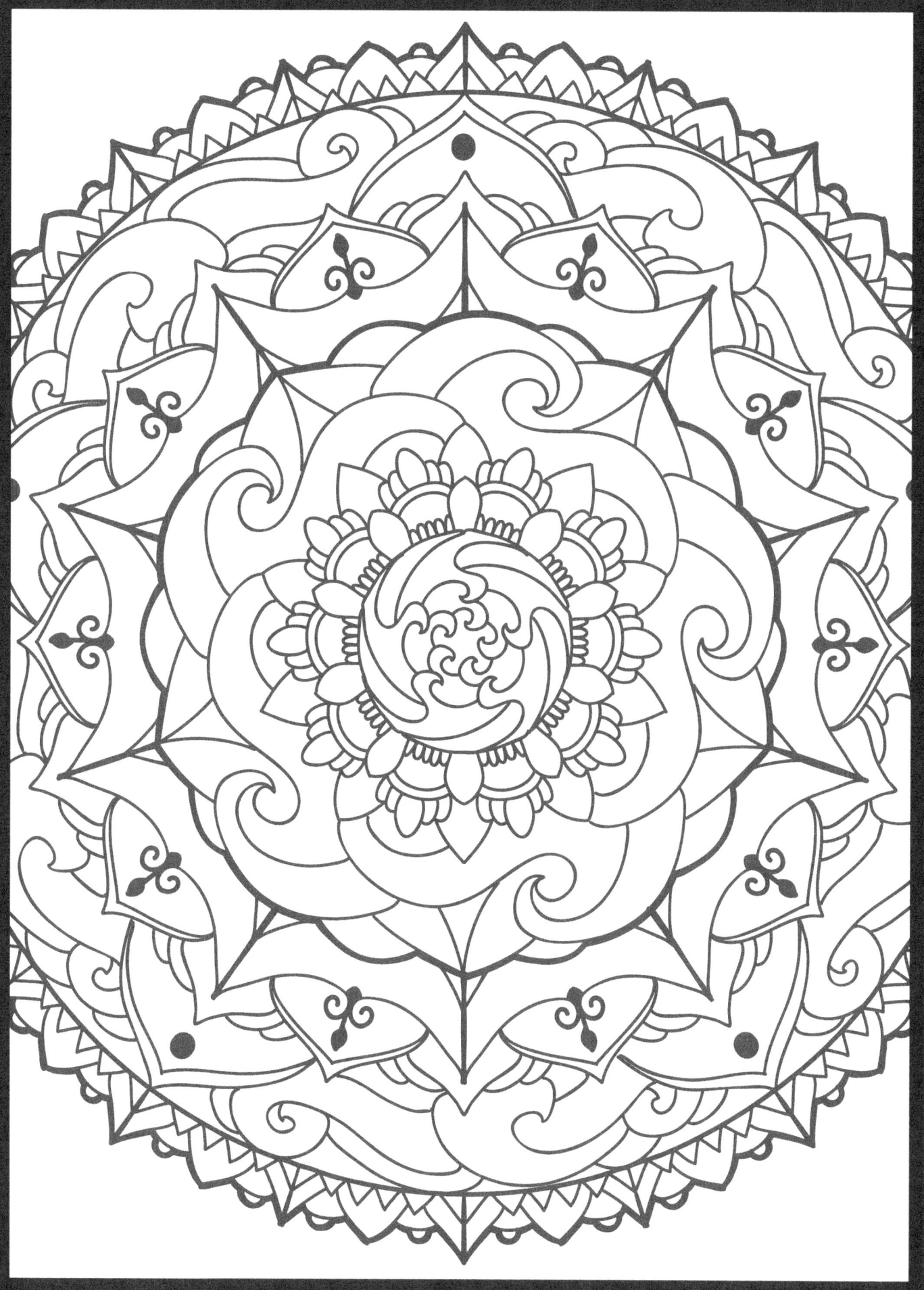

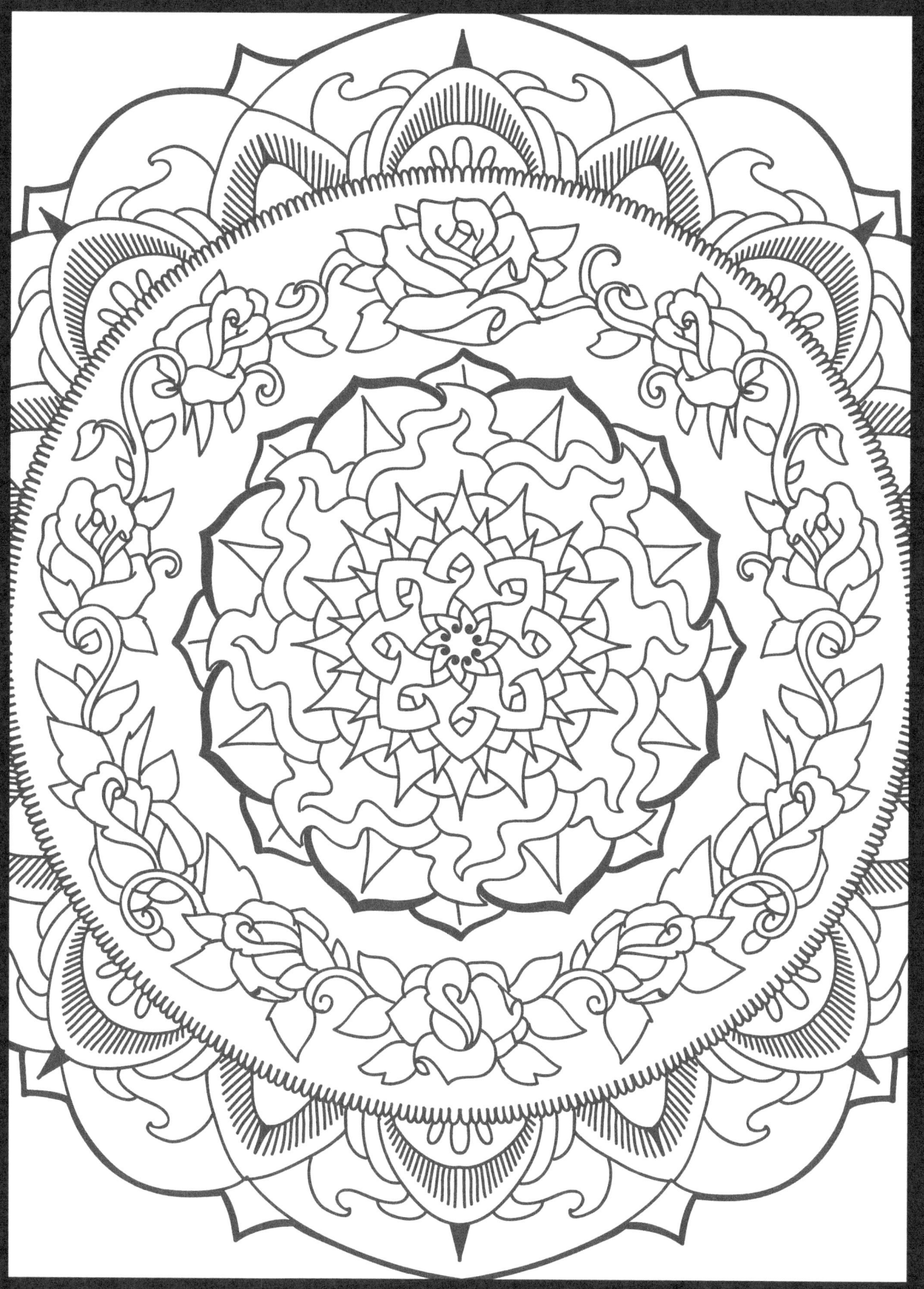

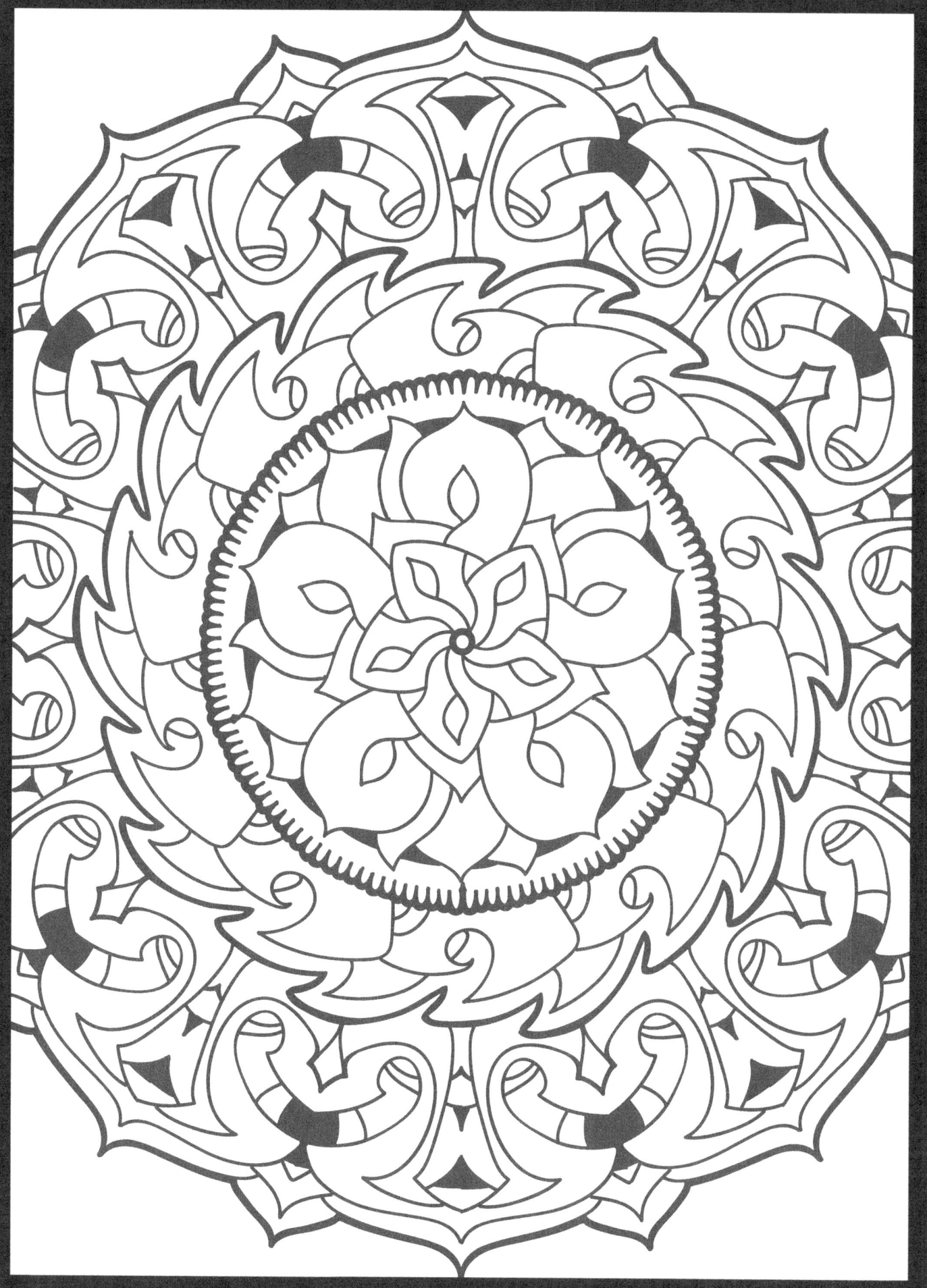

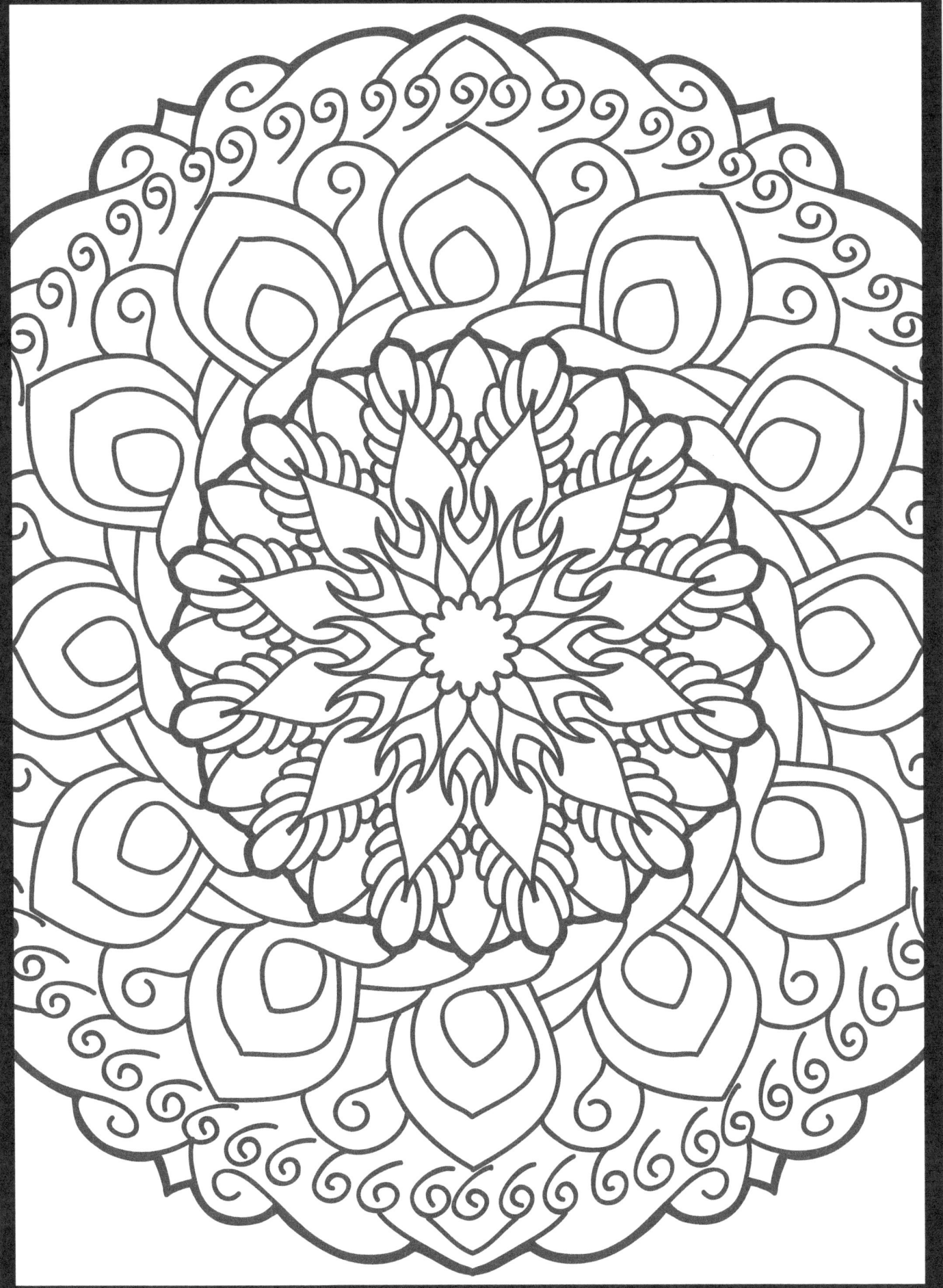

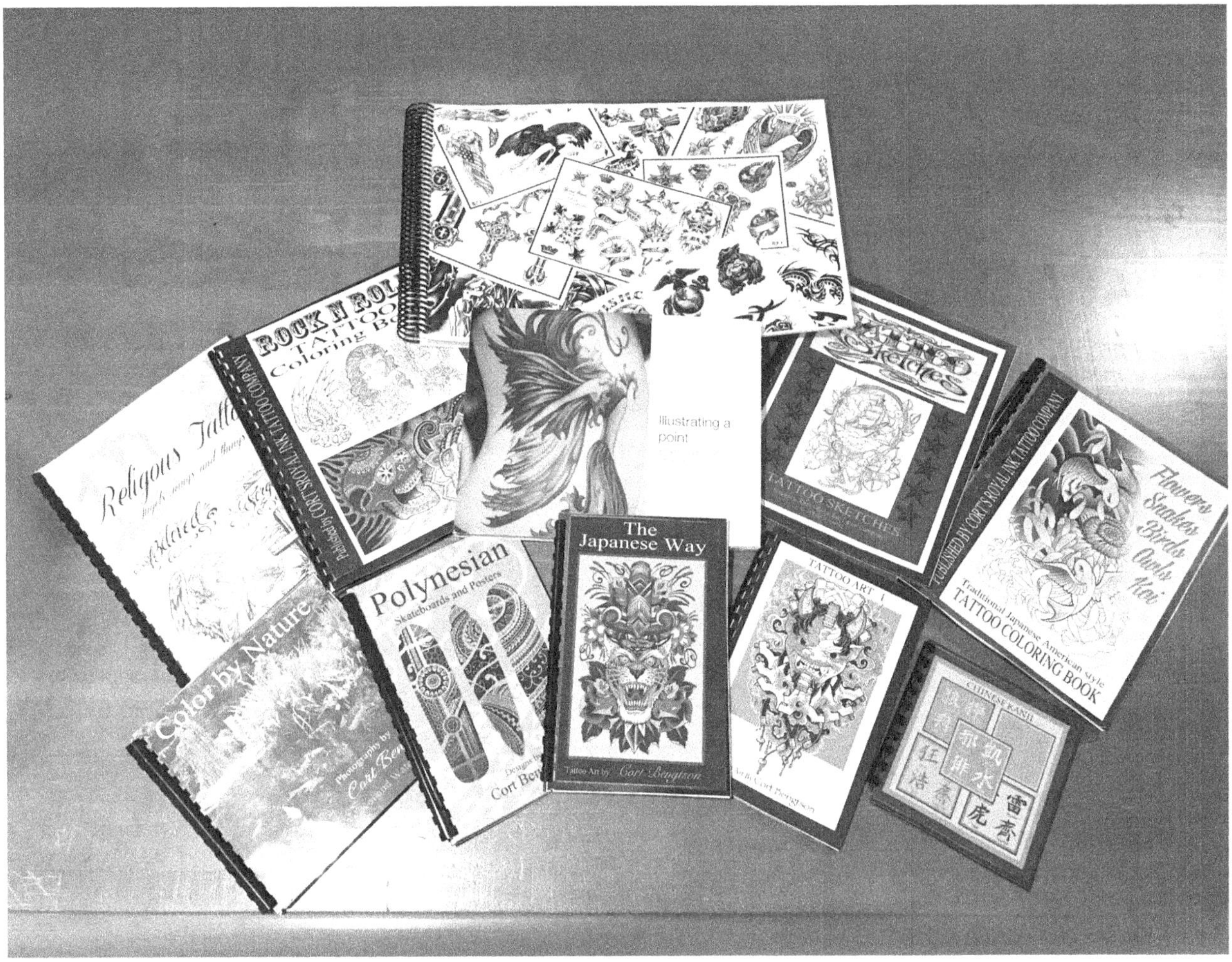

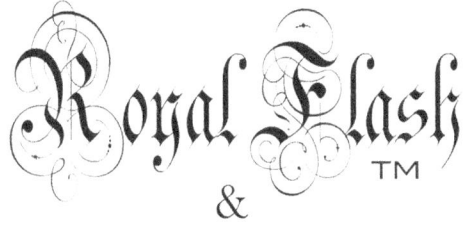

From Japanese style to surreal black and gray, to watercolors and computer art, we have something you will love. Prints ranging in size from 11" x 17" to 40" x 50" will adjust the visual appeal of any room.

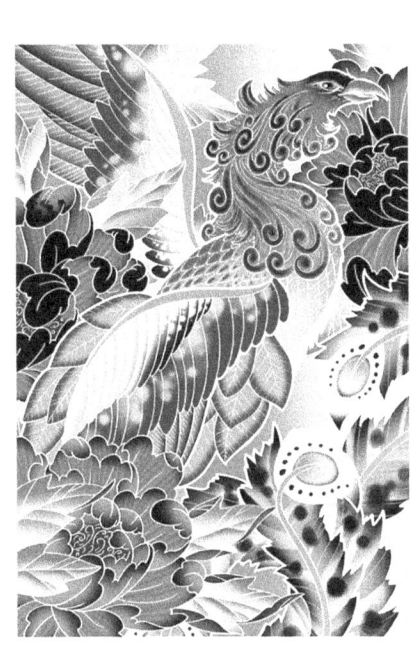
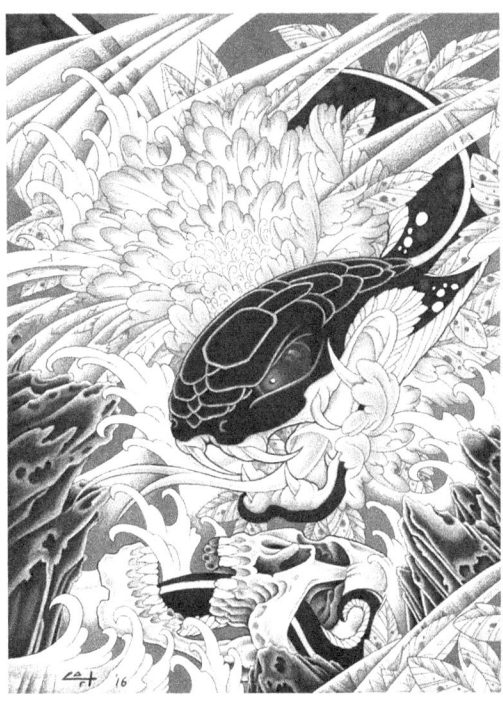
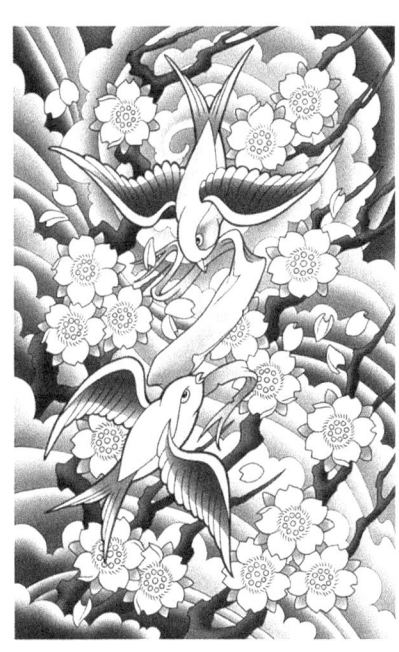
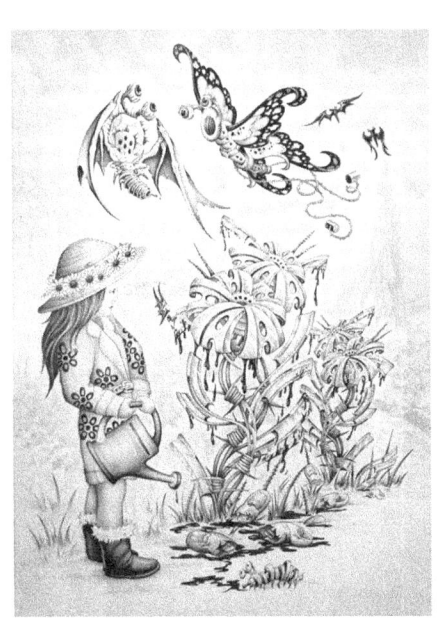
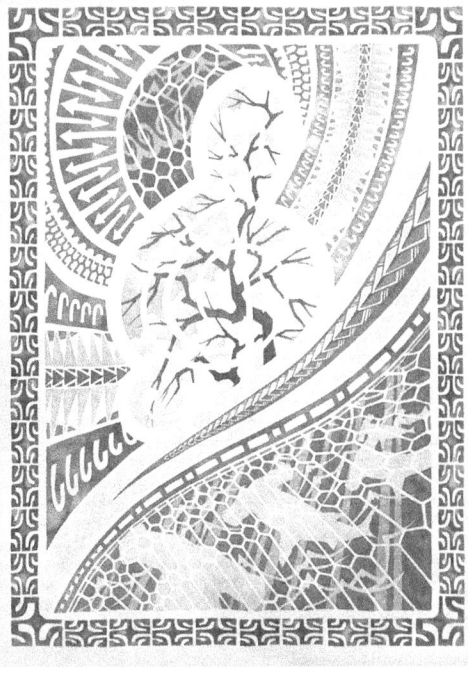
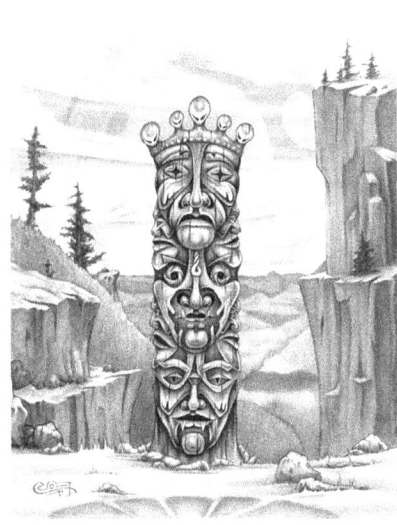

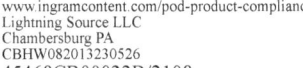